Index to

POLITICAL

SERMONS

OF THE

AMERICAN

FOUNDING

ERA

1730–1805

Edited by Ellis Sandoz

LIBERTY FUND
Indianapolis

Index to Political sermons
of the American founding

Inc., a foundation established to
free and responsible individuals.

The cuneiform inscription that serves as our logo and as the design motif for
our endpapers is the earliest-known written appearance of the word "freedom"
(amagi), or "liberty." It is taken from a clay document written about 2300 B.C. in
the Sumerian city-state of Lagash

PRINTED IN THE UNITED STATES OF AMERICA

97 98 99 00 01 P 5 4 3 2 1

LIBRARY OF CONGRESS CATALOGING-IN-PUBLICATION DATA

Index to Political sermons of the American founding era, 1730–1805
    edited by Ellis Sandoz.
        p.   cm.
    ISBN 0-86597-151-X
    1. Political sermons of the American founding era, 1730–1805—
Indexes.   2. Christianity and politics—United States—Sermons—
Indexes. 3. United States—Politics and government—Sermons—Indexes.
4. Sermons, American—Indexes.
I. Sandoz, Ellis, 1931–   . II. Political Sermons of the American found-
ing era, 1730–1805.
BR115.P7P53 1997   97-3500
261.7'0973'09033—DC21

LIBERTY FUND, INC.
8335 Allison Pointe Trail, Suite 300
Indianapolis, IN 46250-1687
(317) 842-0880

Contents

Subject Index

Aaron
  church-state relations and, 1118,
    1127, 1495
  as God's minister, 342–43
  inspiration of, 1117
  law and, 340*n*
  Moses and, 1105, 1127, 1326, 1443
  prayer and, 36
  as priest, 1106
  wilderness and, 1420
Abed-nego, 590
Abel, 312, 536, 567, 590, 1487
Abel, city of, 755
Abimelech, 592, 753, 953
Abner, 1399, 1400, 1402
Abolitionism, 1049*n*, 1053, 1054, 1203.
  See also Slavery of Negroes
Abraham
  angels and, 1379
  blessings of, 1034, 1038
  chosen people of God and, 1460
  covenant of circumcision and, 340
  descendents of, 1221
  divine providence and, 593
  God's cause and, 590
  God's omnipotent spirit and, 592
  heights of, 799
  Isaac and, 1500, 1581
  Jesus Christ's kingdom and, 204

Lot and, 751
  sons of, 1033
Abrahamic covenant, 1033
Absalom (Absolom), 668, 722
Absolute government, 805, 808,
    871–72, 1054, 1176, 1179. *See also*
    Arbitrary government; Tyranny
Abyssinia, 1047
Achilles, 1205
An Act for the better securing the
    Dependency of his Majesty's
    Dominions in America upon the
    Crown and Parliament of Great-
    Britain, 277
Adam, 203, 538*n*, 584, 1051, 1195, 1457
Adams, John
  aristocracy and, 1288–89, 1495, 1501,
    1519–21, 1527
  British party and, 1522*n*
  days of prayer, fasting, and
    thanksgiving proclamations,
    xxiii, 1340
  Duffield and, 772
  elections and, 1494, 1498, 1501, 1525
  Fenno and, 1527*n*
  France and, 1523, 1527
  gratitude for, 1334
  Hamilton and, 1522
  inflexibility of, 1552
  inspiration from, 1569
  liberty and, 1499–1500, 1526

Adams, John, *continued*
Peabody and, 1322
portrayals of, 688
respect for, 701
trade and commerce and, 699
United States Constitution and, 1483, 1519–20
as United States President, 1344–45
worship and, 1469
Adams, Samuel, 646n, 942, 1102, 1218
Addison, Joseph, 598, 899
Adonibezek, 716
Adrian, 1392
Adultery, 1499n, 1511
Advent
destruction of world and, 1585
divine judgment and, 1582, 1585, 1586, 1587
doctrine of, 1583
first advent of Jesus Christ, 1579, 1582, 1585–86
Jehovah and, 1582–83
prophecies of, 1587–88
second advent of Jesus Christ, 999, 1393, 1579, 1582, 1588–90, 1592, 1595
Aeneas, 1200, 1205
Africa and Africans. See also Negroes; Slavery of Negroes; Slave trade
Abraham's blessing and, 1038
Christian conversion of, 1048–49, 1049n, 1051
colonies of, 272, 284, 1040, 1041
conquest of, 1050
Dana's African Slave Trade, 1031–55
development of, 1049n
Great Britain and, 567
liberty and, 1160

origin of mankind and, 1505
Portugal and, 1038, 1040, 1042
slavery of Negroes and, 1042, 1046, 1051, 1052, 1392, 1507–8
slave trade history, 1038–47
war in, 1047
African Americans. *See* Negroes
The African Slave Trade (Dana), 1031–55
Agincourt, battle of, 547n
Agriculture
encouragement of, 939, 1564
feudal system and, 1250
French Revolution and, 1239, 1248–49
United States government and, 1228
Washington and, 1405, 1407
Ahab (king), 320, 323, 598, 724
Ahasuerus, 592, 665, 758
Ahaz (king of Israel), 315–16, 320
Ahithophel, 130, 418, 669
Aix Chappelle, peace of, 478
Ajalon, 593
Albert de Capitaneis, 747
Albigenses, 204, 502n, 748
Alceus, 1552
Alcoran, 1083, 1093
Alembert, Jean le Rond d', 1372, 1372n
Alexander, Archibald, 1150
Alexander the Great, 761, 993, 1399, 1409
Alien and Sedition Acts, 1342, 1520
Allegiance, 451–54, 485, 489
Allen, John
biographical information on, 302
Oration upon the Beauties of Liberty, 303–25

Almon, John, 4242

Alous, sons of, 1380

Alphonsus (king of Arragon), 747

Alphonsus (king of Portugal), 1039, 1040

Alphonsus III (king of Arragon), 748

Alva, Fernando Alvarez de Toledo, Duke of, 502*n*, 676

Amalek, 572

Amalekites, 583

Amaziah, 756, 763

Ambrose, 746

American Academy of Arts and Sciences, 649*n*, 1130

American Indians. *See* Indians

American Mother club, 1383

American Revolution. *See also* British army and navy; Colonial America; Colonial militia
arbitrary power and, 597
British Crown and, 475, 489, 490
British ministry and, 692, 972, 997
British Parliament and, 492, 599
Case's *Defensive Arms Vindicated*, 713–70
cause of God and, 595, 603, 779, 1173
charters and charter rights and, 637–38, 870
Christian church and, 522*n*
Church of England and, 1491
church-state relations and, 1118
civil liberties and, 872
civil society/civil union and, 874
as civil war, 520
colonial America's cause and, 601–5, 640–42, 726, 756, 780
colonial America's successes and God, 625, 787, 800

colonial militia's lack of preparation for, 672–73, 778, 800
commemorations of, 612, 621, 658
Committees of Safety and, 1284–85
Cumings's *Sermon Preached at Lexington on the 19th of April*, 659–81
days of prayer, fasting, and thanksgiving proclamations, xxiii–xxiv
defense and, 640, 642, 756, 799, 1390–91
divine providence and, 958, 1334, 1436
Duffield's *Sermon Preached on a Day of Thanksgiving*, 773–88
effects of, 600–601, 1565
equality and, 1051, 1311
evils and, 856
God and, 522–23*n*, 549, 618, 720, 798–801
Great Britain's inadequate representation and, 1024
Great Britain's justification for, 571–72
Great Britain's management of, 550–51
Great Britain's waging war against her children, 597, 602
Great Britain's wrath as cause of, 673–74
happiness of posterity and, 878
history of, 719–20, 1173–74
liberty and, 778, 1053, 1313, 1314
military forces of, xvi
ministers and, xiii, 779, 862, 1315
need for, 443, 1563–64
Paris peace treaty of 1783, xvi, 530
patriotism and, 850, 874
peace contrasted with, 1335
poverty and, 875

American Revolution, *continued*
  prevention of, by colonial assemblies, 603
  principles of, *595*
  public expenses of, 938
  religion and, *551–52, 600*
  rights and, 1316
  as self-defense, 799
  selfish motives of, *551–52*
  union of the people and, 874
  United States' commitment to, *651–52, 1358*
  Washington and, 1407
  wrath of men and, 669–70, 672
America's Appeal to the Impartial World (Moses), 441–92
Ammianus Marcellinus, *543*
Ammon, 33, 753–54
Ammonites, 757, 856, 953
Anabaptists, 364, 1083
Anarchy
  Christianity and, 1158
  dangers of, 852
  as extreme, 1334
  factions and, 1294
  in France, 1298, 1358, 1360
  justice and, 147
  liberty and, 1016, 1180
  patriotism and, 1320
  republican governments and, 1176, 1319
  tyranny and, 1428
Anaxagoras, 1182
Andes, 1454, 1455, 1456*n*
Andrews, Bishop, 820*n*
Andross, Sir Edmond, 512
Angels
  Abraham and, 1379
  American Revolution and, 523*n*
  angel of death, 974

Babylon's fall and, 500
  care of man and, 889–90
  fallen angels, 191–92
  God's attributes and, 979, 981
  happiness and, 892
  Jesus Christ and, 190–91
  reason and, 896
  rulers as wise as, 15
  seraphim, 981
  soldiers of Jesus Christ and, 194–95
  war of, 506, 574
Anger. *See* Wrath of men
Anglican Church. *See* Church of England
Angola, 1041*n*
Ann (Queen of England), 596
Annapolis, Nova Scotia, 477–78
Anspach, 781
Anthony, 1204
Antichrist
  destruction of, 999, 1098
  doctrines of, 127–28
  empire of, 1367, 1369–71, 1393, 1515
  French Revolution and, 1353, 1353*n*
  governmental authority and, 20
  Jesus Christ's kingdom and, 729
  kingdom of, 893
  religion and, 728
  rules to Christians and, 76
  second advent and, 1590
  Waldenses and, 747
Antigua, 1042, 1043*n*
Antinomian morality, 208
Antioch, 856
Antiochus Epiphanes, 744
Apal Relat, 731
Apis, 1198
Apocalypse. *See* Second advent

Apostles
  advent and, 1590
  gifts of, 204
  Jesus Christ as king and, 188
  as Jesus Christ's soldiers, 196
  Jesus Christ's suffering and, 993
  obedience and, 1071
  as pillars, 14
  rulers as God's ministers and, 1433
Apostles' Creed, xxi
*An Appeal to the Public for Religious
  Liberty* (Backus), 329–68
Application, xxi, xxii
Arabs, 1010, 1050, 1508
Arbitrary government. *See also*
  Absolute government; Tyranny
  administration of, 437
  defensive arms and, 733
  in Europe, 1311
  fear and, 1179
  Glorious Revolution and, 994,
    1009
  independence and, 1560
  laws of God and, 59
  liberty and, 443
  submission to, 1053
Architectural metaphor, pillars as,
  12, 14
Ardres, 1041n
Areopagus, 1259
Arian heresy, 746, 1083
Aristides, 928
Aristocracy. *See also* Monarchy
  Adams and, 1288–89, 1495, 1501,
    1519–21, 1527
  balance of power and, 1176–77
  in Europe, 1288–89
  Fenno and, 1524
  as form of government, 1083, 1327
  French Revolution and, 1248

  hereditary rulers and, 1435, 1519
  influence and, 1289–91
  natural, 920–21, 1288–89
  Pinckney and, 1495
  societies as, 1233, 1279
  United States and, 1289
  United States President and, 1290
Aristotle, 134, 1204
Ark of the covenant, 595
Armada, 134, 544
Armageddon, 1368
Armenians, 746
Armies. *See* British army and navy;
  Colonial militia; Military
  forces; United States army
Arminianism, 120, 208, 658, 1023n, 1170
Armon, 756
Arnisaeus de author Prici, 731, 732
Arnold, Benedict, 700, 1069
Arnold, Welcome, 1174n
Arragon, 748
Artaxerxes, 592, 756–57
Articles of Religion, 74
Artillery sermons
  as sermon type, xxiii
  Sewall and, 26
  Thacher's *Sermon Preached Before
    the Artillery Company*, 1131–47
Arts
  church-state relations and, 1122
  flourishing of, 1337, 1575
  French Revolution and, 1250–51
  Greece and, 1016
  happiness and, 1071
  printing and, 987
  societies and, 1279
  support of, 1077
  United States government and,
    649, 899–900, 1314

Asa (king), 211, 212, 218, 223, 594

Asahel, 1399

Asaph, Bishop of, 476, 601

Asaph the Psalmist, 583

Asher, 759

Ashfield, 349–54, 353n, 364, 368

Ashteroth, 954

Asia
  Greece and, 805
  liberty and, 1160
  luxuries of, 853
  Mithridates and, 1281
  origin of man and, 1505, 1506
  Roman conquest of, 804
  Sulla and, 1282

Askelon, 1402

Assassinations, 1203–4, 1265, 1374

Assyria, 593, 594, 786, 1050

Assyria, king of, 403, 666, 794, 798, 955

Athaliah, 756

Athanasius, 746, 1491

Atheism
  church-state relations and, 1494
  civil injuries and, 1516
  civil society/civil union and, 1461
  dignity of man and, 894
  education and, 1376
  enemies of Jesus Christ and, 1382
  Europe and, 1400
  France and, 1252, 1253, 1262, 1265, 1266, 1268
  French Revolution and, 1269, 1270, 1291, 1348
  God and, 1126
  immortality of soul and, 1400
  infidelity and, 1464
  Jefferson and, 1461–62, 1467, 1470, 1517n

religion as protection against, 1380
  resistance to, 1388
  Roman Catholic Church and, 1355n, 1360
  rulers and, 1328
  spread of, 1473–74
  true religion and, 895
  Voltaire and, 1372

Athens, 808, 856, 950, 1177, 1201, 1259, 1335

Atkinson Academy, 1322

Attila (king of the Huns), 1247, 1346

Attleborough, 360

Auckland, Lord, 1526n, 1528

Auctoritas patrum, 921

Augustine, Saint, xxi, 715

Augustus (emperor of Rome), 993

Austria
  antichristian empire and, 1371, 1393
  defensive arms and, 749
  French Revolution and, 1246, 1267, 1271
  house of, 748
  Jews in, 1392
  Russians and, 997
  Switzerland and, 594–95

Austrian Succession, War of, 123–36

Authority
  Christianity and, 990, 1538
  citizens and, 307–8, 1021
  disregard of, 852
  of God, 382, 1191
  of Jesus Christ, 64, 67, 87–88, 90, 117, 1037, 1093
  of kings, 315, 323, 767
  laws and, 467–69
  of magistrates, 724–25
  of reason, 1191
  religious establishments and, 67–72, 966, 989–92, 1015

of rulers, 20, 21, 1037, 1421, 1422
support of, 923
unjust, 1334
Avignon, 1352n, 1371
Aylmer, 95
Azariah, 756

Baal, 954
Babel, 829, 892
Babylon
    dignity of man and, 892, 895
    divine providence and, 593
    fall of, 500, 588, 842, 856, 1367–68
    in figurative sense, 1367–68, 1576
    Jews and, 40, 216, 617, 631–33, 761,
        795, 954, 956–57
    oppression of, 193
    pride and, 567
    rise of, 813
    slavery and, 1051
    Whore of Babylon, 357n, 499, 515,
        1354–55n
Bacchinalia, 1195
Bacchus, 1257
Backus, Isaac
    Appeal to the Public for Religious
        Liberty, 329–68
    Baptist Church and, 328, 330, 367,
        368
    biographical information on, 328,
        330
    Leland and, 328, 1080
Bacon, Francis, 897
Bacon, Leonard, 1030
Bailyn, Bernard, xxiv, 302
Bajazet, 750
Baker, Frank, 410, 412
Balaam, 216
Balance of power in Europe, 1271

Balance of power in government,
    487, 802, 1176–77, 1343–44
Baltimore, Maryland
    Smith's Sermon Preached Before a
        Convention of the Episcopal
        Church, 817–34
Banquo, 1501
Bantam, 750
Baptism, 339–40, 344, 361n, 1170
Baptists and Baptist Church. See also
    Pedobaptism
    Allen and, 302
    of Ashfield, 353n
    Backus and, 328, 330, 367, 368
    British constitution and, 348–62
    Leland and, 1080
    in Massachusetts, 344
    ministers' salaries and, 348, 355
    peace in civil state and, 93
    role of, 328
Barak, 751, 752, 786
Barantenes (king of Persia), 746
Barbadoes, 1042, 1043n, 1047, 1048
Barclay, 731
Barrack, 1403
Barré, Isaac, 476
Barrere, 1281, 1284
Barruel, Abbe, 1355n, 1376n
Basil, 746
Batavia, 1384, 1385, 1390, 1393
Baxter, Andrew, 898
Beast. See also Dragon; Satan;
    Serpent
    dragon and, 520
    horns of, 517
    interpretation of, 525–27
    mark of, 20
    number of, 527

Beast, *continued*
  Roman Catholic Church and,
    501–2, 502*n*, 525, 1368
  tyranny and, 504, 518
Beauzet, Mr., 1372*n*
Bedford, New York, 730
Belcher, Joseph, 360
Belgium, 1351, 1371, 1384, 1385, 1390, 1393
Belial, 1474
Belial, sons of, 346, 570–71, 760
Belknap, Dr., 1354–55*n*
Bellamy, Joseph, 440, 884, 1030, 1186, 1416
Bellingham, 357
Belsham, Thomas, 970
Belshazzar, 592
Benevolence
  Christianity and, 1113, 1550
  civil liberties and, 1158–59
  civil officers and, 1069
  of God, 1013
  gratitude to God and, 879
  liberty and, 992
  national happiness and, 875–76
  in politics, 1115
  principle of universal benevo-
    lence, 1010, 1011, 1025, 1063, 1540
  revenge and, 1533, 1535
  of rulers, 1332
  societies and, 1279
  tendency toward good and, 1208
Benin, 1040, 1041*n*
Benjamin, 230, 763
Benjaminites, 570–71, 953, 1429
Berenger, 640
Berens, John F., 1102
Berkley, 1552
Bernard, 512

Bethel, 320
Bethlehem, 993
Beziers, Earl of, 748
Bible. *See* Gospel; Prophets and
  prophecies; Scriptures; specific
  biblical figures; and Biblical
  Citation Index
The Bible and the Sword (Fletcher),
    561–78
Bible religion, 1087–88
Bibulus, 1522, 1522*n*
Biddle, 785
Bigotry, 1181, 1254, 1257, 1264, 1275
Bill of Rights, xvi, 599, 1080
Bills of credit, 173–74
Bishop, 706
Bishop, Right Rev., 1343
Blacks. *See* Negroes
Blackstone, William, 449
Blair, 1404
Blakeney, 132
Bland, 132
Blasphemy, 948
Blessings
  of Abraham, 1034, 1038
  conduct and, 853–57
  of gospel, 863
  government as, 936, 1317
  gratitude to God and, 1358
  of human nature, 1012–16
  of Jews, 124, 614
  national, 1381
Blind guides, 1095, 1095*n*
Blind man, 1052
Bloody tenet washed, 345*n*
Blount, William, 1465
Bodin, Jean, 712
Bodin de Repub., 731

Bohemia, 205, 519, 747, 750

Bojador, Cape, 1038

Bolingbroke, Lord. *See* St. John, Henry

Bondage. *See* headings beginning with slavery

Bond-woman, children of, 1033, 1035, 1050

Boniface IV, 1257

Borgia, 691

Boston, Massachusetts
Allen's *Oration upon the Beauties of Liberty*, 303–25
American Revolution, battles of, 781, 1567
Anonymous's *Dialogue Between the Devil, and George III, Tyrant of Britain*, 689–710
Boston Massacre sermons, xxiv
British march from, 622
Colman's *Government the Pillar of the Earth*, 9–24
Cooper's *Sermon on the Day of the Commencement of the Constitution*, 629–56
Cumings's *Sermon Preached at Lexington on the 19th of April*, 659–81
East Indian Company tea, 482, 570–71, 573
Emerson's *Oration in Commemoration of the Anniversary of American Independence*, 1557–69
evacuation of, 547
harbor closure, 399, 570
infant baptism and, 347
Mayhew's *Snare Broken*, 233–64
oppression of, 743, 756, 758, 779n
Osgood's *Wonderful Works of God Are to Be Remembered*, 1219–34
problems of, 377, 402, 481

Sewall's *Nineveh's Repentance and Deliverance*, 27–50

Tappan's *Sermon for the Day of General Election*, 1103–27

Thacher's *Sermon Preached Before the Artillery Company*, 1131–47

Thayer's *Discourse Delivered at the Roman Catholic Church in Boston*, 1341–61

Boulanger, 1473

Bourbon, Cardinal, 715

Bourbon, house of, 243, 651, 1497

Bowdoin, James, 608

Bowen, Ephraim, 1174n

Bradock, 1407

Bradstreet, Simon, 52

Brandywine, 787

Brazil, 1040, 1041

Breda, treaty at, 477

Brenna, 748

Bridenbaugh, Carl, xiv

Briggs, John, 623

Brissot de Warville, Jacques-Pierre, 1263, 1269–70, 1295, 1297

Brissotines, 1269–70, 1297

Bristol, England
slave trade and, 1043
Wesley's *Calm Address to Our American Colonies*, 411–20

Britain's Mercies, and Britain's Duties (Whitefield), 121–36

British army and navy
conduct of, 556, 566, 621, 622, 622n, 625, 625n
failure of, 707
flight of, 547, 597, 623n
hostility toward colonial America, 483–84
Indians and, 625, 625n, 641

British army and navy, *continued*
  justification of, 574–75
  naval superiority of, 654, 672,
    697–98, 778, 800
  oppression of, 622, 654
  strength of, 778
  training of, 799–800
British colonies. *See also* Colonial
  America; and names of specific
  colonies
  British liberties and, 270
  British Parliament and, 269–77,
    273, 282, 413, 691
  charters and charter rights and,
    413–16
  elections and, 414–15, 419, 430
  Johnson's definition of, 425
  natural rights and, 414
  obedience of, 271
British constitution
  Baptists and, 348–62
  British Parliament and, 273–74,
    276, 281, 283, 456, 487
  colonial America and, 422, 461,
    472–73, 599
  free government of, 424
  Great Britain at war with, 1559
  legislative power and, 295
  liberty and, 273, 286, 290–91,
    297–98, 427, 476, 871
  perversions of, 436–37
  Puritans and, 1116*n*
  religious liberty and, 342–48
  representation and, 270–71, 285,
    1023–24
  rights and, 446–47
  Scotland and, 395–96
  sovereignty of the people and, 308
  taxation and, 270, 284–86, 290, 291,
    297, 419, 433, 447, 487
  trial by jury and, 449

United States Constitution and,
  998
Virginia and, 460–61
British Crown
  absolute monarchy, desire for, 777,
    1562–63
  attitude toward colonial America,
    484–85
  charters and charter rights and,
    752, 1562
  claim to colonial America, 311, 322,
    468
  colonial America's loyalty to, 296,
    313, 325, 381, 397*n*, 399, 474–75,
    671, 720
  colonial America's slavery and,
    776
  colonial constitutions and, 468,
    470–72
  dependency on, 279–80, 295
  elections and, 293
  enemies of, 416–17, 422
  Gaspee affair and, 306–7, 310
  grants and patents from, 457
  as head of church, 480
  influence of, 436
  obedience to, 286
  rights of, 307
  role of, 316–17
  taxation and, 284–85, 287, 290–91,
    294
  treatment of colonial America,
    461, 464
  war against colonial America, 475,
    489, 490
British House of Commons
  authority of, 461, 464–65, 475
  British Crown and, 436
  Charles I and, 596
  colonial America's cause and, 601
  fishing rights and, 462

as part of British Parliament and,
253
representation and, 1023–24
righteousness and, 147
taxation and, 285, 286, 288–89,
292–93, 295, 429, 433, 448
toleration and, 1022*n*

British House of Lords
British Parliament and, 253
Charles I and, 596
colonial America's cause and, 601
representation and, 322
righteousness and, 147
taxation and, 286
toleration and, 1022*n*

British ministry
advice of, 705
American Revolution and, 692,
972, 997
blunders of, 695
charters and charter rights and,
401
colonial America as enslaved and,
313, 621
crimes of, 709, 1565
Gaspee affair and, 307, 310, 311
judges and, 319
liberty and, 597
liberty of conscience and, 403
lies of, 701
rebellion's cure and, 699

British Parliament
American Revolution and, 492,
599
authority of, 270, 271, 273–76, 279,
281, 291, 446
British colonies and, 269–77, 282,
413, 691
British constitution and, 273–74,
276, 281, 283, 456, 487
British Crown's desire for absolute
monarchy and, 777, 1562–63

charters and charter rights,
253–54, 415–16, 599
Church of England's doctrine
and, 1022*n*, 1023*n*, 1263
colonial America as subjects and,
451
colonial America's cause and, 601
colonial America's enslavement
and, 240, 245–46, 691, 776
colonial America's independence
from, 474–75, 491–92
colonial America's supporters in,
256–57, 799
dependency on, 279
England and, 275, 282
Ireland and, 275–76, 282, 464
jurisdiction of, 462, 464–65, 467,
468, 470–74
laws and, 274, 279, 282, 322, 379*n*,
400, 487, 492, 599, 799
obedience to, 454
oppression of, 513
peace and, 258, 298–99
power and, 621, 958
property and, 290–91
Roman Catholic Church and, 502
taxation and, 253, 279, 281–82,
287–88, 292, 294, 295, 298, 353,
397*n*, 428
toleration and, 1022*n*, 1023*n*
trade and commerce and, 1562
Zubly's *Humble Enquiry into the
Nature of the Dependency of the
American Colonies upon the
Parliament of Great Britain*,
267–99

British party, 1498, 1501, 1522*n*, 1526,
1527–28

Brown, Charles Brockden, 1478

Brown, Dr., 1312*n*

Brown, Francis, 623

Brown, John, 1178*n*

Brunswick, 701

Brutus, 1141, 1206, 1440

Buchanan, George, 722, 724

Bumsted, John M., 302

Bunker Hill, battle of, 692, 799

Buonaparte, 1352, 1522n, 1524n

Burdens of citizens, 881, 930, 937–38, 959, 965

Burgoyne, John, 625, 692

Burke, Edmund, xiv, 422, 424, 476, 651, 1006, 1008

Burnet, Bishop, 316

Burr, Aaron, Sr., 180

Bute, John Stuart, Earl of, 323, 691, 695, 704–6

Butler, 825n

Butterfield, Lyman H., 1082

Byril, 746

Cabindo, 1041n

Cabot, Sebastian, 454

Caesar, Julius, 200, 320, 993, 1482, 1522n

Caesarea Philippi, 1134

Caesars, Washington compared with, 1399

Cain, 19, 360, 536, 590

Caleb, 932

Calendar, France's changing of, 1258, 1262

California, 1505

Caligula (emperor of Rome), 691, 694, 1090

Calixtus III, 1039

A Calm Address to Our American Colonies (Wesley), 411–20, 422

Calvin, John, xxi, 204, 330, 1491

Calvinism, 120, 208, 1023n, 1263. See also Protestants and Protestantism

Cambambe, 1041n

Cambyses (monarch of Persia), 1198

Camden, Lord, 602

Canaan and Canaanites
    courts and, 947
    Dan and, 1134
    divine providence and, 593
    evil reports of, 932
    idolatry and, 954
    Jews and, 507, 751, 797, 1050, 1105, 1392
    Joshua and, 786
    kings of, 759, 768
    righteousness lacking in, 567, 804
    road to, 476

Canada, 246, 477, 480

Cape-Breton, 478

Capernaum, 128

Carey, Matthew, 1453n

Carlton, 512

Carolina, 781

Carrier, 1384

Carthage, 810, 856

Case, Stephen
    biographical information on, 712
    Defensive Arms Vindicated, 713–70

Cassius, 1440

Catalinarian conspiracy, 928

Cataline, 1202, 1525n

Catawba, 781

Catherine of Medicis, 1293

Catholic Church. See Roman Catholic Church

Cato, 1141, 1200, 1200n, 1201n, 1206, 1523

Cause of God
  colonial America's cause and, 595,
    603, 779, 1173
  divine truth and, 584
  doctrines as, 584
  God's pleading of, 587–95, 604–5
  manifestations of, 843
  universal righteousness and,
    584–85, 596
  welfare of people as, 585–87
Cayenne, 1043n
A Century Sermon on the Glorious
  Revolution (Winchester),
  971–1000
Century sermons
  Glorious Revolution and, xxiii,
    970
  Winchester's Century Sermon on the
    Glorious Revolution, 971–1000
Cere, 340n
Ceremonial law, 1062
Certificate law, 1093–94, 1097, 1098
Cesar (emperor of Rome), 1205
Cesarea, 746
Chalcol, 891
Chaldeans, 23, 219, 891, 898, 1383
Chapin, Nathan, 355
Charitable Fire Society, 1130
Charity
  abolition of slavery and, 1054
  Christianity and, 826, 828, 832–33,
    1183, 1483
  liberality of sentiment and,
    1428–29
  societies and, 1279
  true religion and, 895
Charlemagne, 750
Charles I (king of England)
  authority of, 323
  Cromwell and, 1283–84
  execution of, xxiii, 307, 317, 692
  fishing rights and, 462
  French Protestants and, 750
  liberty and, 320
  taxation and, 448
  tyranny of, 596, 691, 704
Charles II (king of England)
  Connecticut and, 1092, 1093
  liberty and, 320
  liberty of conscience and, 988
  piracy and, 462
  power of, 438, 1334
  swearing of, 695
  tyranny of, 750
  Virginia and, 461–62
Charles IX (king of France), 1293
Charles V, Duke of Saxony, 748
Charleston, South Carolina, 410
Charlestown, 625n, 1140
Charters and charter rights
  American Revolution and, 637–38,
    870
  Ashfield and, 351n
  Backus and, 330
  of Boston, 399, 752
  breaking of charters, 735, 752
  British colonies and, 413–16
  British Parliament and, 253–54,
    415–16, 599
  of colonial America, 272, 294, 295,
    398, 870
  of Connecticut, 1092, 1093
  fishing rights and, 462
  ineffectiveness of, 640
  of Ireland, 279, 397n
  king and, 470, 1562
  liberty and, 402, 728
  liberty of conscience and, 344,
    364
  of Massachusetts-Bay colony, 416,
    420, 432–33

Charters and charter rights,
continued
of New England, 169–70
of Pennsylvania, 415–16, 420, 432
Protestants and, 343–44
religion and, 359, 1093
of Rhode Island, 305
rights antecedent to, 445–56
rights of British subjects and,
457–58
rights subsequent to, 456–76
threats to, 377, 381, 400, 420

Charybdis, 1229, 1259, 1526

Chase, Samuel, 266

Chastity, 1200–1201, 1374

Chatham, Earl of. *See* Pitt, William

Chauncy, Charles
baptism and, 361*n*
biographical information on, 138
*Civil Magistrates Must Be Just,
Ruling in the Fear of God*, 139–77

Chebucto, 1391

Chedarlaomer, 751

Chelmsford, 355

Cheronae, 1526

Chevrus, Rev., 1349*n*

Children. *See also* Parents; Youth
of bond-woman, 1033, 1035, 1050
Christianity and, 1114
conscience and, 1085–86
education of, 163, 918, 939, 961,
1073–74, 1077, 1440, 1442
heathens and, 1204
honor to parents and, 1432
morality of, 880
obedience and, 1360–61
parents' conduct and, 905
people as children, 1070
prayer for parents, 1353
resistance of, 737, 740

as rulers, 1422
as slaves, 1204
of Sparta, 1202
subordination of, 452–53, 1430–31,
1433, 1442
training of, 878, 880, 905, 961

Chillingworth, 1573

Choissey, General, 782

Chosen people of God. *See also* Jews
delivering themselves from
oppression, 764
divine providence and, 1211, 1419–20
Dunbar's *Presence of God with His
People*, 209–30
God's vengeance for, 617–18, 621
Jefferson and, 1460, 1460–61*n*, 1462
Keteltas's *God Arising and Pleading
His People's Cause*, 581–605
prophecies and, 612–13
punishment of, 615
true religion and, 797
Zion as, 586, 604

Chrasroes (king of Persia), 747

Christ. *See* Jesus Christ

Christian church. *See also* Church of
England; Ministers; Protestants
and Protestantism; and specific
denominations
American Revolution and, 522*n*
Bohemia and, 519, 747
building up of, 829
corruption of, 617, 823–24, 1487
creeds of, 1589–90, 1595
decline in doctrine and, 523–24
defensive arms of, 729
divine providence and, 521–24, 613
divine revelation and, 1578
enemies of, 617
faith and, 830
fall in regard of, 843
indifference of members, 831

Jesus Christ as mediator for, 813
Judaism distinguished from, 1033,
    1579–80
martyrs of, 842
Messiah and, 1579
persecutions and, 842
safety of, 510–12
Sherwood's *Church's Flight into the
    Wilderness: An Address on the
    Times*, 485–527
state of, 503–4, 508
theology and, 1589
trials and sufferings of, 507, 518–19,
    521
triumph of, 620
in United States, 804
wilderness and, 508–9, 522
woman as symbol for, 505, 509, 519,
    524
Christian denominations. *See*
    Protestants and Protestantism;
    and specific denominations
Christianity and Christians. *See also*
    Christian Church; Persecutions;
    Protestants and Protestantism;
    Roman Catholic Church; and
    headings beginning with
    Ecclesiastical
advent and, 1594
Africans and, 1048–49, 1049*n*, 1051
anarchy and, 1158
arguments of infidels and, 1492–93
authority and, 990, 1538
benevolence and, 1113, 1550
ceremonial rites of, 1114
charity and, 826, 828, 832–33, 1183,
    1483
citizens as Christians, 1495–98
civil liberties and, 125
civil officers as Christians, 1098
in colonial America, 1380
conduct and, 1310
conscience and, 1157
Constantine the Great and,
    989–90
corruption and, 1159–60, 1488, 1515
defensive arms and, 747–48
despotism and, 1156, 1157, 1161
disciples of Christ as Christians,
    64
disputes within, 825–26, 1586
duty and, 1113, 1158, 1207, 1209, 1482,
    1484–98
education and, 1212
Edwards's *Necessity of the Belief of
    Christianity and Christians*,
    1187–1216
enemies of, 745, 1452
enslaved by Muhammadanism,
    1263
Ethiopia and, 1161*n*
external evidence of, 994, 995
facts of, 993–94
free inquiry and, 1515
French Revolution and, 1164–65*n*,
    1266, 1270
future state of existence and, 1207,
    1209–10
golden rule of, 1158
governmental influence of, 1155
happiness and, 1124
heathens and, 1051
history of, 993–94
humanity of, 1204
hypocrisy and, 1468–69, 1484
infidelity and, 990, 1192–93, 1469,
    1474
Jacobin Society and, 1239, 1253,
    1257, 1291
Jefferson and, 1454, 1460, 1464,
    1465, 1473, 1483, 1499
knowledge of, 1115
laws against, 388

Christianity and Christians, *continued*
  liberty and, 597–99, 1036, 1154–60,
    1163, 1167
  liberty of conscience and, 1035
  love and, 830, 1011
  magistrates and, 1211–13
  maxims of, 996
  morality and, 1113, 1166, 1183, 1189, 1191,
    1196
  nations and, 1160–62
  opposition to, 1213
  oppression and, 1156, 1163
  paganism and, 519, 990, 1194–96,
    1485
  passions of men and, 1310
  patriotism and, 1011, 1166
  persecutions and, 1159*n*, 1197–99,
    1489
  philosophical religion compared
    with, 1192–93, 1207–11
  piety and, 1192
  prevalence of, without aid of law,
    1086
  principles and rules of, 378
  prosperity and, 842, 1189, 1206, 1212,
    1213
  religious establishments and, 1083
  resistance of, 745–50
  right of private judgment and,
    1054
  rights and, 1036, 1156, 1432
  Roman Catholic Church's spread
    and, 499–503
  Romans and, 519, 728
  Sabbath and, 1380
  sciences and, 1585
  scriptures and, 62, 74–76, 90, 1456,
    1582
  security of, 1483
  self-denial and, 557
  slavery as tyranny and, 1156, 1160
  slavery of Negroes and, 1046,
    1048, 1049*n*, 1051, 1162*n*
  soul and, 1432
  spirit of, 1037
  suffrage and, 1212, 1215–16, 1465
  tolerance and, 1491–92
  tyranny and, 1158, 1550
  union of, 825
  United States and, 830, 831, 1166,
    1392, 1550–51
  United States Constitution and,
    1500, 1525
  unity of judgment and, 825
  universal dominion of, 1162–63
  usefulness of, 1207–11
  vice and, 1199–1206
  vindication of, 1489
  virtue and, 832, 1156, 1332, 1438
  Voltaire and, 1372–73, 1464, 1465
  war and, 576
Chronologies
  1688–1773, 3–6
  1774–1781, 369–72
  1782–1788, 683–86
  1789–1794, 1001–4
  1795–1805, 1301–4
Chrysippus, 1200
Chrysostom, 746
Church buildings, destruction dur-
    ing American Revolution,
    600–601, 730
Churches. *See* Christian Church;
    Christianity and Christians;
    Protestants and Protestantism;
    Roman Catholic Church; and
    specific denominations
Church government
  civil government and, 335–48
  civil rulers and, 71–72, 102–5

ecclesiastical constitutions, 108–9, 128, 274, 1325
ecclesiastical laws, 274, 276
Churchill, John, Duke of Marlborough, 1399
Church-Men, 93
Church of England
  in Colonial America, 120, 232
  evangelism of, 232
  George II and, 125
  persecutions and, 1491
  religious establishment and, 1083, 1491
  religious modalities and, 68
  Scotland and, 1023
  Smith and, 816
  southern states and, 1083
  toleration and, 1022, 1022*n*
  uniformity of practice in religion and, 91
  in United States, 1491
  Wesley and, 410
Church officers. *See* Ministers
The Church's Flight into the Wilderness: An Address on the Times (Sherwood), 493–527
Church-state relations. *See also* Religious establishments; Religious liberty; Right of private judgment; Toleration
  Aaron and, 1118, 1127, 1495
  arts and, 1122
  Backus and, 328, 330, 345
  Baptists and, 352
  civil power over religion, 648, 1516–18
  colonial ancestors and, 1118
  cooperation and, 1114
  corruption and, 1492, 1493
  in France, 1252
  Great Britain and, 990

history and, 1117–19
Israel and, 950
Judaism and, 945–46, 950, 955, 957
liberty and, 1126
liberty of conscience and, 339, 990
religion as pillar of government, 22, 1126
separation of, 1482, 1487–90, 1516
taxation and, 363–64, 368
tolerance and, 1491
union and, 1494, 1495, 1495*n*
United States Constitution and, 1494
Williams's *Essential Rights and Liberties of Protestants*, 53–118
worship and, 365–66
Wortman and, 1482, 1487–90
Cicero
  civil liberties and, 258
  Delphic oracle and, 1256
  driven from Rome, 928
  gentleness of, 1141
  murder of, 1204
  as philosopher, 134, 854, 1255
  quoted, 375, 1237
  Rome and, 1202
  vice and, 1200*n*, 1201
  Washington's death and, 1399
Cimbri, 1282
Cincinnati Society, 1407, 1413
Cinna, 1282
Circumcision, covenant of, 340
Citizens
  body politic compared to human body, 386, 391, 677
Citizens and citizenship. *See also* Patriotism
  agreement in government, 914
  authority and, 307–8, 1021

Citizens and citizenship, *continued*
    burdens of, 881, 930, 937–38, 959,
        965
    citizenship of Jews, 1392
    complaints of, 930–31
    cooperation with rulers and, 1386
    equal influence over free govern-
        ment, 1279, 1280
    of Great Britain, 997
    happiness of, 1067
    honesty of, 1541–43
    immunities of, 1182
    ministers' duties as, 1494
    national character and, 1551–52
    National Convention of France's
        use of citizen, 1260
    obedience to laws, 1070–71, 1496
    obedience to magistrates, 741, 922,
        1116, 1430, 1432
    patriotism of, 1125
    removing to another kingdom or
        country, 452–53
    representatives' dependence on,
        1435
    responsibilities of, 961, 1433
    righteousness of, 933, 965
    rights of, 1260, 1260n
    training of, 918, 1117
    virtue of, 877, 1337–38, 1435
    of world, 1012, 1025
Civil authority. *See* Authority
Civil government. *See* Government
Civil laws. *See* Laws
Civil liberties
    American Revolution and, 872
    benevolence and, 1158–59
    of Christians, 125
    civil society/civil union and, 1068
    in colonial America, 258–61
    Connecticut's legislature and, 859
    constitutions and, 636, 644

divine providence and, 1227
    in France, 997
    James II and, 157
    justice and, 156–62, 172
    licentiousness and, 1179
    nonconformists and, 1083
    principles of, 1064–68
    religious establishments and, 1489
    religious liberty and, 549, 558,
        734–35, 1495
    of Romans, 158
    slavery and, 1054
    Tammany Society and, 1154
    tolerance and, 1490–91
    tyranny and, 1061–62
    United States and, 783, 833, 1441
    Washington and, 1405
Civil Magistrates Must Be Just,
    Ruling in the Fear of God
    (Chauncy), 139–77
Civil officers. *See also* Magistrates
    choice of, 1066
    Christianity and, 1213
    of Connecticut, 858, 1436
    duties of, 1329–30, 1338
    election of, 1069–70
    heresies and, 1514
    infidelity and, 1468
    informed opinions of, 1386
    Ireland and, 1023
    private interests and, 1069
    religious establishment and, 1083,
        1088, 1098
    taxation and, 1067
    Test Laws and, 1022, 1022n
    vice and, 1070
    virtue of, 1069, 1070, 1116, 1120, 1122,
        1335
Civil rights. *See* Civil liberties
Civil rulers. *See* Kings; Rulers

Civil society/civil union. *See also*
    Government
    American Revolution and, 874
    atheism and, 1461
    benefits of, 382
    civil liberties and, 1068
    of colonial America, 496, 504, 552
    of colonial America with Great
        Britain, 578
    constitutions and, 923
    defense and, 1387
    disorders of, 387
    dissolution of, 388
    as duty, 1385–87
    factions and, 928
    Goodrich's *Principles of Civil
        Society and Happiness Considered
        and Recommended*, 911–40
    gospel and, 923–24
    government and, 382, 1268, 1298,
        1385–86
    happiness and, 915, 932, 1157
    Illuminati and, 1374
    internal civil union, 874–75, 879
    Israel's laws and, 948
    Jerusalem and, 913
    laws of, 65–66, 383, 386, 917, 923
    laws of God and, 914–18
    laws of nature and, 917
    ministers and, 935
    national union and, 929
    natural equity and, 428
    necessity of, 486, 876
    peace and, 936
    principles of, 914–19
    property and, 429
    rational liberty and, 915–16
    reciprocal support and protection,
        875
    religion and, 919–20, 923, 939, 1113,
        1124
    rights of, 429, 456

    sin and, 934–35
    taxation and, 347–48
    voluntary agreement of, 383
Civil wars, 520, 1231, 1280, 1292, 1295,
    1299, 1536. *See also* American
    Revolution; French Revolution;
    Rebellion; Revolutions
Clark, 749
Clark, Charles E., 302
Clark, Mr., 347n
Clark, Rev. Mr., 621n
Clergy. *See* Ministers
Clinton, George, 702
Clinton, Sir Henry, 692, 694, 696,
    704
Clive, Robert, 1047
Clodius, 1202
Cloots, Anarchalis, 1497
Cloud of glory, 976
Cobbett, 1526, 1526n, 1528
Coke, Lord, 426
Coligni, Gaspard de Châtillon, 749
Colleges and universities, 163, 169,
    1121–22. *See also* Education
Colman, Benjamin
    biographical information on, 8
    Cooper and, 628
    Government the Pillar of the Earth,
        8–24
    Great Awakening and, xvii
Colonial America. *See also* American
    Revolution; Colonial assem-
    blies; Plantations; Taxation of
    colonial America; Trade and
    commerce; and headings begin-
    ning with United States
    attacks on, 416
    British army's and navy's hostility
        toward, 483–84

Colonial America, *continued*
British constitution and, 422, 461,
472–73, 599
British Crown's claim to, 311
British Parliament's absolute
power and, 958
British Parliament's constitutional
power and, 273–74, 276
British Parliament's power to
enslave, 240, 245–46, 691
British Parliament's power to legislate for colonial America, 279,
322, 397*n*, 400, 599, 799
British Parliament's power to tax
and, 279, 281–82, 295, 298, 397*n*
charters and charter rights,
253–54, 272, 294, 295, 398, 870
Christianity in, 1380
Church of England in, 120, 138
civil liberties in, 258–61
colonial America's cause and, 601,
640–42, 726, 756, 780
common cause, 404–7
as creditors to Great Britain, 479
David and Goliath compared to
colonial America and Great
Britain, 799
defense of, 443, 463–64, 475–76
dependence on Great Britain, 272,
277–81, 290, 295
differences among the people in,
778, 800
distance from Great Britain, 490,
550
as distinct state from Great
Britain, 472
divine providence and, 546–48
duties and, 324
enemies of, 257–58, 476–77, 720
enemies of British Crown and, 417
as English subjects, 445, 451–56,
460
Europe and, 183, 246, 504

France and, 198, 203, 240, 245, 246,
255
French and Indian Wars, 477–78
government of, 240, 404–6,
490–91, 778, 800
Great Britain's advantages and,
477–79
Great Britain's demands on,
476–85
Great Britain's national debt and,
777
Great Britain's oppression and,
250, 399, 778, 1563
Great Britain's supporters of,
256–57, 604, 640–42, 799
growth of, 241, 242
independence from Parliament,
474–75, 491–92
independent nationhood and, xvi,
291, 417
Indians and, 240, 245, 1198
internal policy of, 397*n*, 490
internal polity of, 430, 551
James II and, 397*n*
jealousies within, 261–62
justification for resistance, 731
laws of, 308
laws of nature and, 310
liberties of, 306, 312, 481
liberty and, 240, 241, 292, 378,
419–20
loyalty to British Crown, 70, 296,
313, 325, 381, 397*n*, 399, 474–75, 671
Magna Charta and, 240, 426
Mather's *America's Appeal to the
Impartial World*, 441–92
military preparedness of, 1140
moderation and Great Britain,
252–58
Native American wars and, 477
natural rights of, 444–45
as part of Great Britain, 272
peace among ourselves and, 403–7

peace between colonial America and Parliament, 258, 298–99

petitions to Great Britain, 240, 241, 248, 260–61, 708, 720, 799

Pitt and, 235–36

population of, 504, 565n

rebellion and, 310, 323, 489, 697, 722

reformation and, 338–39

representatives of, 322

revenue for Great Britain, 1560–61

rights antecedent to charters or colonial constitutions, 445–56

rights of, 308, 481

rights subsequent to charters and colonial constitutions, 456–76

rivalries of, 379, 403–4, 491, 1276

Roman Catholic Church and, 502n

settlement of, 455

slave trade and, 1041n

Spain and, 255

Stamp Act and, 238–39, 241, 244–49

subjects' rights and, 450–51, 457, 460

submission to Great Britain, 778

territorial encroachments and, 211–12

treaties with Great Britain, 491–92

union of, 496, 504, 552, 800

wars against foreign nations and, 235

as wilderness for Christian church, 503–4, 508, 1117

Zubly's *Humble Enquiry into the Nature of the Dependency of the American Colonies upon the Parliament of Great Britain*, 267–99

Colonial America as enslaved. *See also* Slavery as tyranny

British Crown's plan for, 693, 705, 776

British ministry's vengeance and, 313, 621

British Parliament and, 240, 245–46, 691, 776

Great Britain's reconciliation terms and, 491

liberty and, 258, 259

patriots counteracting, 248, 801

property and, 474

rights and, 310, 322, 377, 443

taxation and, 291, 420

as uniting factor in American Revolution, 1284–85

Washington's saving from, 745

Colonial ancestors

church-state relations and, 1118

divine providence and, 1313–14

freedom and, 639, 1546

liberty and, 1312, 1546, 1567

persecutions and, 1515–16

public days of devotion and, 1224

religious liberty and, 363, 508, 568, 872–73, 1117, 1546

republican government and, 1546–47

rights and, 1312

as subjects, 445

Colonial assemblies

British Parliament's authority and, 279, 464

constitutions for, 491

as Houses of Representatives, 280, 1562

internal policy, 430, 490

legislation and, 464

prevention of American Revolution, 603

William Smith and, 816

Colonial assemblies, *continued*
suspension of, 280, 298
taxation and, 277–78, 291, 294, 295, 469
Colonial constitutions
British constitution, similarities with, 461, 472–73
British Parliament's jurisdiction and, 470–71
for colonial assemblies, 491
consent and, 480
defense and, 463
intent of, 458–59, 465–66
king's right of sovereignty and, 468
made by and with king, 470–72
rights antecedent to, 445–56
rights subsequent to, 456–76
Colonial militia
expenses of, 938
Great Britain and, 1140
internal liberty and, 681
lack of preparedness of, 672–73, 778, 800
lawfulness of defensive arms and, 717
lusts of men and, 680
Massachusetts military forces and, 1135
patriotism of, 679, 779
payments to, 846
relationship to God and, 623–24, 717–18
successes of, 625, 625n
tories' view of, 753
vice and, 718
Washington and, 786
Colonial sympathizers in Great Britain, 256–57, 517, 640–42, 799
Colonies. *See* British colonies; Colonial America; Portugal
Colossus, 1491

Commerce. *See* Trade and commerce
Common cause
of colonial America, 404–7
sympathy of, 1451
Common debts
taxation and, 346
Common-prayer, book of, 1083
Commons. *See* British House of Commons
Common Sense, 538–39n, 717, 1474
Commonwealth government, 418, 436
Communion, and Moses Mather, 440
Compacts. *See* Constitutions
Concord, Battle of, xxiv
Conde, Louis I de, 749
Conduct
accountability for, 1191
blessings and, 853–57
of British army and navy, 556, 566, 621, 622, 622n
Christianity and, 1310
citizens' burden and, 937
error in, 1543
as good policy, 1537–38
gospel and, 1452
grievances and, 937
of Jefferson, 1464
of Jesus Christ, 1537–40, 1543–45
laws of God and, 1466
of Moses, 977
prudent conduct, 552
public conduct, 1115–16, 1117, 1553
religion and, 1115, 1117
of rulers, 1425
ten commandments and, 946
virtue and, 965
of Washington, 1404–5, 1407

Confirmatio Cartarum, 447

Confucius, 1255

Congo, 1040, 1041*n*

Congregationalists and Congregationalism, 8, 93, 138, 530

Congregationalist Standing Order, 1080

Congress. *See* Continental Congress; United States Congress

Connecticut. *See also* Hartford, Connecticut; New Haven, Connecticut
  charter of, 1092, 1093
  civil officers of, 858, 1436
  election sermons preached in, xxii
  health and, 1225
  Leland's *Rights of Conscience Inalienable*, 1081–99
  manumission and, 1053
  ministers of, 861–62
  Moses's *America's Appeal to the Impartial World*, 441–92
  piracy and, 462
  population breakdown of, 1045*n*
  religious establishment in, 1086, 1091–99
  religious liberty in, 1080
  Sherman's *Scriptural Instructions to Civil Rulers*, 375–407
  slave population of, 1045*n*
  Williams's *Essential Rights and Liberties of Protestants*, 53–118

Connecticut Society for the Promotion of Freedom, 1030

Conscience. *See also* Liberty of conscience
  children and, 1085–86
  Christianity and, 1157
  compact and, 1085–86
  definition of, 1085
  dominion of, 1027
  fundamental laws and, 918
  Glorious Revolution and, 1020
  God and, 225, 1062, 1064, 1068, 1085, 1467
  holiness and, 891–92
  of Jefferson, 1467–68
  Jesus Christ as Lord of, 65–67
  justice and, 1063, 1429
  magistrates and, 925, 931
  patriotism and, 931
  personal influence and, 1291
  rebellion and, 323
  religion and, 1087, 1110–11
  religious liberty and, 740, 873, 1064
  right of private judgment and, 1063
  rights of, 62, 73, 116, 127
  rulers and, 176, 392
  scriptures and, 66, 1596
  subjection to magistrates and, 722
  true religion and, 1064
  tyranny and, 1061
  virtue and, 1337
  worship and, 97, 101–2, 644

Consent
  constitutional, 480
  government and, 492, 634–35, 1062, 1066
  Jews and, 634–35
  laws and, 413–14, 427, 1066
  taxation and, 349, 413, 419, 447, 451, 1067
  tyranny and, 474

Constantine I (emperor of Rome)
  Christian church and, 204
  church-state relations and, 1487
  defensive arms and, 750
  gladiators and, 1206
  heretics and, 338

Constantine I, *continued*
prosperity of Christianity and, 842
religious establishment and, 989–90, 1083, 1088–89
Constantinople, 746
Constantius, 746
A Constitutional Answer to Wesley's Calm Address (Anonymous), 423–38
Constitutions. *See also* British constitution; Colonial constitutions; United States Constitution
advantage of framing of, 794
altering of, by legislators, 1085
American Revolution's protection of, 651–52
benevolence and, 1158
civil societies and, 923
conscience and, 1085–86
consent and, 480
Cooper's *Sermon on the Day of the Commencement of the Constitution,* 629–56
corruption of, xvii–xviii
divine, 382
ecclesiastical, 108–9, 128, 274, 1325
founders of, 653
framing of, 643, 794, 802
of France, 1231, 1297
God's guidance in, 794
government and, 335, 456, 473, 1083–84, 1296
of Israel, 636–37, 645, 946
laws and, 387, 1084–85
liberty and, 728, 1155, 1299
of Massachusetts, 629–56, 1118, 1130
McClintock's *Sermon on Occasion of the Commencement of the New-Hampshire Constitution,* 791–813
obedience to God and, 811
passions of men and, 1299
privilege of, 935–36
revision of, 1331
right of self-defense and, 736
right to be governed by, 1064
rulers and, 146–47, 381
spirit of, 811
of states, 958, 998, 1098
tyranny and, 959
violations of, 456–57
weakness in government and, 1421–22

Continental Congress. *See also* United States Congress
Adams and, 699
American Revolution markers and, 782n
Backus and, 328
confederation and, 958
days of prayer, fasting, and thanksgiving proclamations, xxiii–xxiv
Duffield and, 772
free trade and, 516
God's aid to, 779n
resistance and, 799
retaliation law and, 522
Witherspoon and, 530
Zubly and, 266

Convention sermons, xxiii

Cook, James, 1505

Cooke, Daniel, 1174n

Cooke, Rev. Mr., 621n

Cooper, Samuel
biographical information on, 628
A Sermon on the Day of the Commencement of the Constitution, 629–56

Cooper, William, 628

Copeland, Thomas W., 1008

Copernicus, 1182

Cornbury, Lord, 512

Cornelius, 576

Cornwallis, Charles Cornwall, 1st Marquess, 688, 697, 698, 703, 704, 782

Corruption
of Christian church, 823–24, 1487
Christianity and, 1159–60, 1488, 1515
church-state relations and, 1492, 1493
of doctrine, 842
of government, 1024
Jesus Christ's gospel and, 822–23
Jews and, 823
of Judaism, 1034
in judges, 960, 1520
liberty and, 334
of luxury, 1077, 1390
of morality, 841, 842
tyranny and, 1155
wealth and, 842

Cotton, James, 52

Cotton, John, xxiii, 344*n*, 345*n*

Cotton, Josiah, 361

Country. *See also* Nations; Patriotism
definition of, 1009
duty to, 557, 742–43, 1009
partiality of, 1009–10
rights of, 1012, 1025

Court of Inquisition, 96

Courts. *See also* Judges
appeals to higher court, 932, 947
balanced powers of, 802, 1176, 1343
cases of inconsiderable value and, 951, 966
courts of admiralty, 307, 315, 318, 322, 324, 450
decisions of, 1423
independence of, 1520
in Israel's government, 947, 953, 956
oppression and, 1442

plea in court, 733
private debts and, 1423–24

Covenants
Abrahamic covenant, 1033
consent of Jews and, 634–35
covenant of circumcision, 340
keeping covenant with God, 220–22
personal and corporate, xv

Cowpens, 781

Cowper, William, 1051*n*

Creation as work of God, 1221

Creatures, 611, 793–94, 879, 889, 890

Credit. *See* Public credit

Cretans, 1201

Crete, king of, 1185

Cromwell, Oliver, 544, 566, 1268, 1283–84, 1486*n*

Cross as weapon, 202

Cruckshank, 719

Cruelty, 992, 1203

Crumpond, New York, 730

Cuba, 478

Cueta, Africa, 1038

Cumberland, Duke of, 132, 162

Cumings, Henry
biographical information on, 658
Sermon Preached at Lexington on the 19th of April, 659–81

Currency. *See* Money

Curse of Meroz, 721, 759, 785, 1138

Cushan-rishathaim (king of Mesopotamia), 751

Cushing, Jacob
biographical information on, 608
Divine Judgments upon Tyrants, 609–26

Cushing, Thomas, 608

Custine, Adam Philippe, Comte de, 1376
Cyaxares, 1368
Cyder Act, 296
Cyrus, 362, 592, 786, 798, 985, 1368

Daggett, David, 836
Dan
  Abraham and, 751
  idolatry and, 954
  Jeroboam and, 320
  Laish and, 1134–35, 1139, 1143, 1383
  neglecting duty to resistance and, 759
Dana, James
  African Slave Trade, 1031–55
  biographical information on, 1030
Dana, Samuel Whittelsey, 1030
Danforth, John, 360
The Dangers of Our National Prosperity; and the Way to Avoid Them (Wales), 837–63
Danican, General, 1384
Daniel
  Adams compared to, 701
  dignity of man and, 895
  divine providence and, 593
  God pleading cause and, 590
  Jesus Christ as king and, 187–88
  laws and, 335
  prayer and, 35
  Roman Catholic Church and, 499
  vision of stone and, 813
Danton, Georges Jacques, 1259, 1260n, 1263, 1270, 1284
Darda, 891
Darius, 592, 757, 1368n
Dathan, 780
Davenport, John, 1546

David
  Abner and, 1399
  Absolom and, 668
  colonial America compared to, 799
  death and, 1400
  dignity of man and, 887
  divine providence and, 587, 593
  factions and, 1426
  God and, 583, 978–79
  Goliath and, 548, 754–55, 1315
  house of, 186, 755, 913
  justice and, 141
  laws and, 335
  on mourning, 1402
  nature and, 901
  noble actions and, 893
  Paul and, 1403
  peace and, 939–40
  as pillar, 16, 18
  prayer and, 563
  presence of God and, 224
  quoted, 1397
  rebellion against, 722
  religion and, 895
  as ruler of Israel, 144, 187, 316, 383–84, 955
  Saul and, 727, 755, 766, 901, 1402–3, 1414n
  Solomon and, 904
  truth and, 584
Davies, Samuel
  biographical information on, 180
  Mediatorial Kingdom and Glories of Jesus Christ, 181–206
Davis, Cornelius, 1383n
Davis, John, 350–51, 353n
Davis, President, 1407
de Alvas, D., 749
Dean, 1069

Death
  angel of death, 974
  fall of man in, 1400
  heathens and, 1404
  honoring of, 1402, 1403
  immortality of soul and, 1400
  Jesus Christ's conquering of, 200
  resurrection and, 1401
  as sleep, 1259, 1376
  temporal, 198–99
Deborah, 195, 751, 759
de Buffon, M., 1458
Debts. *See* National debt; Private
  debts
Decii, 197
Declaration of Independence
  colonial ancestors and, 1546
  Continental Congress and, 799
  Jefferson and, 1498
  principles of, 1548
  reasons for, 1173, 1559
  Witherspoon and, 530
Declaration of Rights, 802
Declaratory Act (1766), 266, 733–34
Defense and defensive arms. *See also*
    Military forces; Resistance
  abuse of power and, 720
  alliances and, 1140, 1143
  American Revolution and, 640,
    642, 756, 799, 1390–91
  arbitrary government and, 733
  Case's *Defensive Arms Vindicated*,
    713–70
  Christians' use of, 747–48
  of colonial America, 443, 463–64,
    475–76, 483
  country's distant situation and,
    1143–44, 1390
  as duty, 759–66
  exercises in, 1561

Fletcher's *Bible and the Sword*,
    561–78
  free government and, 1146
  government and, 1141–43, 1433
  independence and, 490
  as instrument of righteousness,
    623
  Jesus Christ and, 764–66
  justification of, 799, 1019, 1077, 1183
  knowledge of war and, 1138
  lawfulness of, 717, 719, 768, 1136–38
  laws of nature and, 263, 481–82,
    726, 734–35, 768
  liberty and, 725, 728, 1135, 1380–81
  Muhammad and the sword, 1093
  nature and, 725, 726
  of New England, 172
  people of God's use of, 744,
    751–58
  of person and property, 57
  Peter and the sword, 727–28
  prayers and tears as, 729
  preparedness for, 1140–41
  private injuries and, 726–27
  property and, 1135, 1388–90
  public expenses and, 1434
  Quakers and, 729
  religion and, 725, 728, 1380–81
  resources for, 490
  self-preservation and, 719, 742
  sudden defense and, 1138–39, 1144
  Thacher's *Sermon Preached Before
    the Artillery Company*, 1131–47
  trifles and, 728–29
  tyranny and, 717, 742
Defensive Arms Vindicated (Case),
    713–70
Deism and deists
  Confucius and, 1255
  as dissenters, 1092, 1095
  Dunbar and, 208
  in France, 1253, 1259

Deism and deists, *continued*
  immortality of soul and, 1400
  Jefferson and, 1473, 1483, 1495, 1499,
    1500–1501, 1517*n*
  morality and, 1207, 1332
  nature and, 1201*n*
  philosophists and, 1373*n*
  religious establishment and, 1088
  religious liberty and, 1098, 1126
  rise of, 990
  Roman Catholic Church and,
    1355*n*, 1360
  United States and, 1191

De Jure regai, 722

Delassart, Mr., 1263

Delaware, 1045*n*

Delaware, Lord, 455

Deliverance
  from enemies, 839–40
  of God, 398–407, 1222
  Jesus Christ's heroic actions and,
    200
  of Jews from Egypt, 973, 974–77
  national, 1224
  Sewall's *Nineveh's Repentance and
    Deliverance*, 27–50

Deluge. *See* Flood

Democracy. *See also* Free govern-
    ment; Republican government
  absolute, 1176
  as form of government, 1084, 1327
  French Revolution and, 1356
  sovereignty of the people and, 1177

Democritus, 1202

Demosthenes, 258, 1257, 1292, 1399,
    1498

Denominations. *See* Protestants and
    Protestantism; and specific
    denominations

Despotism. *See also* Absolute govern-
    ment; Oppression; Tyranny
  absolute, 1176
  balance of power and, 1177
  Christianity and, 1156, 1157, 1161
  France and, 1252, 1297, 1298
  free government compared with,
    925, 1179
  government and, 1019
  liberty and, 1072
  Mexico and, 1160*n*
  Montesquieu on, 1161*n*
  nations and, 1013
  religion and, 1109
  resistance to, 1388
  rights and, 1075
  standing army and, 1267
  United States and, 1390

d'Estaing, Count, 650

Des Trois Pointes, 1041*n*

Destruction
  of antichrist, 999, 1098
  of church buildings, 600–601, 730
  of education, 1182
  of Jerusalem, 40
  of liberty, 1429
  of nations, by God, 796, 1335
  repentance and, 40–44
  of Roman Catholic Church, 515
  of Rome, 1335
  of world, 999, 1585

Dettingen, battle of, 130

Devil. *See* Satan

Dexter, F. B., 866

D'Herbois, Collot, 1295

*A Dialogue Between the Devil, and
    George III, Tyrant of Britain*
    (Anonymous), 689–710

Diderot, Denis, 1372

Dido, 1200

Digby, 698

Dignity of man
  compulsion and, 990
  domination and, 1311
  Emmons's *Dignity of Man*,
    885–907
  God and, 887–90
  happiness and, 892
  holiness and, 891–92
  knowledge and, 890–91, 895–99,
    1071
  noble actions and, 892–93
  parents and, 905–6
  personal dignity, 1193
  religious obligations and, 893–95
  sciences and, 897–98
  soul and, 888–89
  virtue and, 1539
  youth and, 906–7

The Dignity of Man (Emmons),
  885–907

Dioclesian, 192*n*

Diogenes, 906, 1201

Dionysius of Alexandria, 746

Discipline, 1354*n*, 1361

*A Discourse Delivered at the Roman
    Catholic Church in Boston*
    (Thayer), 1341–61

A Discourse on the Love of Our Country
    (Price), 1005–28

Discovery, Europeans' zeal for, 1038

Dissenters
  ministers' salaries and, 1095, 1096
  Protestant Dissenters, 1020, 1021,
    1022, 1022*n*, 1023
  Roman Catholic Church and, 1092,
    1093, 1095

Diversity in religion, 1089

Dives, 1335

Divine judgments
  advent and, 1582, 1585, 1586, 1587
  belief in God and, 32–33
  Canaan and, 1050
  Cushing's *Divine Judgments upon
    Tyrants*, 609–26
  defensive arms and, 726
  on Egypt, 982
  God's omnipotent spirit and, 593
  ignorance of divine judgments,
    620
  indifference to gospel and, 881
  infidelity and, 1475–76
  Jerusalem and, 1439
  Jews and, 666, 788, 795, 1335
  Judah and, 1439
  on nations, 999
  obedience to laws and, 1444
  repentance and, 39–40
  rulers and, 33–36
  United States and, 788, 1439
  variety in, 540
  vials and, 1369–70, 1381
  Washington and, 1439

Divine Judgments upon Tyrants
    (Cushing), 609–26

Divine providence
  American continent and, 1310
  American Revolution and, 958,
    1334, 1436
  attributes of God and, 1222
  belief of, 1191
  chosen people of God and, 1221,
    1419–20
  Christian church and, 521–24, 613
  civil liberties and, 1227
  colonial America's successes and,
    546–48, 625, 787, 800
  colonial ancestors and, 1313–14
  David and, 587, 593
  doctrine of, 533
  examples of, 1391

Divine providence, *continued*
    fishing and, 1225–26
    French Revolution and, 1265
    God's pleading his cause and,
        593–95
    God's rational creatures and, 611
    gratitude to God and, 1316
    harvest and, 1225
    health and, 1224–25
    history and, 544, 1309, 1312, 1314, 1392
    idolatry and, 1221
    independence and, 639, 699, 958
    Israel's government and, 637, 951
    Jews and, 616–17, 758, 975
    lusts of men and, 664
    Madison's *Manifestations of the
        Beneficence of Divine Providence
        Towards America*, 1307–20
    nations and, 795, 813
    New Jerusalem Church and, 1580
    Osgood's *Wonderful Works of God
        Are to Be Remembered*, 1219–34
    peace after American Revolution
        and, 775–76, 958
    perfection of, 620, 624
    power of, 543
    punishment and, 670, 708
    purpose of, 1221–22
    religious liberty and, 1226–27
    as religious principle, 793
    righteous administrations of,
        613–15
    sins and, 1452–53
    Spanish Armada and, 983–85
    trials and, 572
    true religion and, 557–58, 1222
    United States Constitution and,
        957, 997, 1436, 1484
    United States government and,
        1334, 1436–37
    warnings of, 880

    war's successes and failures attrib-
        uted to, 568, 673, 958
    Washington and, 958, 1391, 1405,
        1407
    William III and, 985
    wisdom of, 665
    Witherspoon's *Dominion of
        Providence over the Passions of
        Men*, 531–58
    wrath of men and, 666–69
Divine right of kings doctrine, 383,
    632, 1021, 1176, 1181
Divines. *See* Ministers
Divorce, 1264, 1376
Doctrine
    of advent, 1583
    of antichrist, 127–28
    as cause of God, 584
    of church of England, 1022
    contempt of Christian doctrine,
        1124
    controversies in, 826
    corruption of, 842
    divine right of kings doctrine, 383,
        632, 1021, 1176, 1181
    duty of magistrates to, 1089
    false doctrine, 1369–76
    of final judgment, 1191–92
    of gospel, 1062, 1063
    of Illuminati, 1374
    man's care of himself and, 1378
    of New Jerusalem Church, 1587
    as part of sermon format, xxii
    points of, 829
    of Roman Catholic Church, 65,
        1354*n*
    of salvation, 1462
    of scriptures, 584
Doddridge, Dr., 904
Domination, 536, 1010, 1311, 1312, 1355
Dominico, 1043*n*

The Dominion of Providence over the Passions of Men (Witherspoon), 531–58

Domitian (emperor of Rome), 185*n*, 1488

Double tax, 289–90, 295

Downey, James, xviii

Dragon. *See also* Beast; Satan; Serpent
  beast and, 520
  as cause of dissentions in Christian states, 518–20
  and Christian church, 505–6, 521
  horns of, 515
  perplexity of, 516
  Roman Catholic Church and, 499–500, 506
  tyranny and, 508–10
  woman and, 513, 514, 519

Drahomica (queen of Bohemia), 747

Drinking, excessive, 172–73, 1425

Druids, 1286, 1287

Drummond, Dr., archbishop of York, 1022*n*

Dryden, John, 1557

Duer, Mr., 1522*n*

Duffield, George
  biographical information on, 772
  Sermon Preached on a Day of Thanksgiving, 773–88

Dumouriez, Charles François, 1262–63, 1281, 1286

Dunbar, Samuel
  biographical information on, 208
  Presence of God with His People, 209–30
  published sermons of, xxii–xxiii, 208

Dunmore, John Murray, 512

Dunn, John, 54

Dunster, Henry, 361*n*

Dutch. *See* Netherlands

Duties. *See also* Trade and commerce
  assemblies and, 295
  colonial America and, 324, 469
  taxation and, 285, 292
  Virginia and, 461

Duty
  adherence to, 552–57
  to assert rights, 1311
  Christianity and, 1113, 1158, 1207, 1209, 1482, 1484–98
  civil union as, 1385–87
  to country, 557, 742–43, 1009
  to defensive arms, 759–66
  Dwight's *Duty of Americans, at the Present Crisis*, 1365–94
  firmness in opposition, 1387–91
  to God, 223, 239, 557, 584, 1093, 1320, 1377–91
  government and, 1433, 1441–46
  of gratitude, 1343
  industry and, 556
  to king, 223
  to love, 1093
  magistrates and, 724, 922, 1089
  of man, 832, 1360, 1377–79
  to memories of just, 1402
  of ministers, 1123–25, 1443–44, 1485
  obedience to, 1318
  patriotism and, 1482, 1498–1527
  of people, 863, 1442–43
  philosophical religion and, 1209
  of prayer, 1343
  of preserving Sabbath observation, 1379–81
  public duties of religion, 1014
  to relieve oppressed, 764
  to religion, 742–43
  to rescue, 763–64

Duty, *continued*
    to resist tyranny, 721, 730, 741, 752,
      758–59
    righteousness and, 585
    of rulers, 805–7, 1070, 1327
    scriptures and, 1466
    separation from enemies, 1381–85
    social, 1113–14
    soldiers and, 555–56
    to subordination, 1433
    to support gospel, 1092–93
    to truth, 742
    to United States government, 1343
The Duty of Americans, at the Present
    Crisis (Dwight), 1365–94
Dwight, Timothy
    biographical information on, 1364
    Duty of Americans, at the Present
      Crisis, 1365–94
    Tappan and, 1102

Earle, J. B., 1576
Earth. *See also* World
    Colman's *Government the Pillar of*
      the Earth, 9–24
    destruction of, 999
    judgment of, 1585
    moral earth, 13, 19
    natural earth, 12–13, 19
    second advent and, 1589–90
    woman and, 513, 514
East Florida, 284
East India, 1041
East India Company, 482, 570–71, 573
East Indies, 594, 1040
Ecclesiastical issues. *See* Christian
    church; Church of England;
    Roman Catholic Church

Ecclesiastical leaders, 68, 70–71,
    1105–7, 1114–17, 1122, 1326. *See also*
    Ministers
Edom, 616
Education
    American manners and, 1561, 1568
    atheism and, 894–95, 1376
    of children, 163, 918, 939, 961, 1073,
      1077, 1440, 1441
    Christianity and, 1212
    church-state relations and, 1118, 1122
    colleges and universities, 163, 169,
      1121–22
    destruction of, 1182
    divine providence and, 1223
    in England, 127
    equality in, 1073
    in France, 1251
    government responsibility for, 163,
      169, 366n, 808–9, 861, 905, 1073,
      1331
    happiness and, 1268
    heathens and, 1204–5
    history and, 957
    Illuminati and, 1375
    of Jews, 955–56, 1223
    knowledge and, 878, 880, 961
    laws and, 918
    legislature and, 933, 1121–22
    liberty and, 649
    magistrates' support of, 1116
    in New England, 169
    parents and, 1379
    pedantry and, 903
    philosophy and, 1268
    pious education, 1115, 1116
    religious instruction and instruc-
      tors, 1107, 1111–14, 1123
    support of, 961–62, 1181
    United States government's role
      in, 648–49, 833
    universities and, 1121–22

of Washington, 1405
of youth, 961–62, 1072–73, 1440
Edward, prince of Portugal, 1038,
    1039
Edward I (king of England), 447
Edward IV (king of England), 1040
Edward VI (king of England), 134
Edwards, Jonathan the Elder
    capacities of human mind and,
        898
    Cumings and, 658
    Dana and, 1030
    Davies and, 180
    Duffield and, 772
    Emmons and, 884
    sermon form of, xxii
    Williams and, 52
Edwards, Jonathan the Younger
    biographical information on, 1186
    Dana and, 1030
    Emmons and, 884
    *Necessity of the Belief of
        Christianity*, 1187–1216
Edwards, Sarah Pierpont, 1186
Eglon (king of Moab), 751
Egypt and Egyptians. *See also*
    Pharaoh
    Arabians and, 1050
    arbitrary government and, 1179
    divine judgments and, 982
    divine providence and, 593
    independence and, 489
    Jews' bondage and, 215, 507, 567,
        635, 946, 950, 973
    Jews' deliverance and, 973, 975–77,
        1105, 1419
    Jews' rebellion and, 1476
    Joseph and, 663, 777, 973
    knowledge and, 898
    man's noble actions and, 892
    plagues of, 973–75
    presence of God and, 215, 1392
    slavery and, 215, 507, 567, 635, 946,
        950, 973, 1552
    wisdom of, 891
    worship of cats and, 1256
Ehejah, 978
Ehud, 751
Elect, as chosen people, 586
Elections
    British colonies and, 414–15, 419,
        430
    choice of rulers and, 1327
    church-state relations and, 1494
    dissatisfaction with, 872
    Federalists and, 1498
    freedom of, 1065, 1467, 1471
    frequency of, 1330, 1338, 1435, 1549
    happiness and, 1070
    importance of, 653, 872
    Jefferson and, 1483
    justice and, 1065
    liberty and, 1069–70
    majority versus minority votes,
        1095
    Mason's *Voice of Warning to
        Christians*, 1449–76
    religion and, 1452
    of rulers, 871–72
    standing churches and, 1092
    taxation and representation, 288,
        292–94, 422
    United States Constitution and,
        1498
    of United States President, 1453
    virtue and, 1125
    Wortman's *Solemn Address to
        Christians and Patriots*, 1479–1528

Election sermons
  Chauncy's *Civil Magistrates Must Be Just, Ruling in the Fear of God*, 139–77
  Dunbar's *Presence of God with His People*, 209–30
  Edwards's *Necessity of the Belief of Christianity*, 1187–1216
  Evans's *Sermon Delivered at the Annual Election*, 1059–78
  Goodrich's *Principles of Civil Union and Happiness Considered and Recommended*, 911–40
  Griswold's *Overcoming Evil with Good*, 1531–54
  Langdon's *The Republic of the Israelites an Example to the American States*, 943–67
  McClintock's *Sermon on Occasion of the Commencement of the New-Hampshire Constitution*, 791–813
  Sewall and, 26
  Smalley's *On the Evils of a Weak Government*, 1417–46
  Tappan's *Sermon for the Day of General Election*, 1103–27
  as type of sermon, xii–xiii
  Wales's *Dangers of Our National Prosperity; and the Way to Avoid Them*, 837–63
Electors
  of England, 414, 426, 430, 431
  of Israel, 920–21
  qualifications of rulers and, 1329, 1338, 1435
Eli, 11, 360
Elias, 35
Elijah, 858
Elijah the Tishbite, 598
Eliogabalus, 1488
Elisha, 755

Elizabeth I (queen of England), 750, 983
Embaco, 1041n
Emerson, Ralph Waldo, 1556
Emerson, William
  biographical information on, 1556
  Oration in Commemoration of the Anniversary of American Independence, 1557–69
  Thacher and, 1130
Emmons, Nathanael
  biographical information on, 884
  Dignity of Man, 885–907
  on sermons, xx
  Wales and, 836
Enemies
  to British Crown, 416–17, 422
  character and, 1512–14
  of chosen people of God, 615–18
  of Christian church, 617
  of Christians, 745, 1452
  of colonial America, 257–58, 476–77, 787
  deliverance from, 839–40
  external, 1019
  forgiveness of, 585, 1543
  frailties of, 1540–41
  of God, 1379–80
  to Great Britain, 135, 477
  Indians as, 1175
  internal, 672–73, 1019
  of Jacobin Society, 1242
  Jesus Christ and, 762, 1036, 1039, 1090, 1382, 1472
  kind actions toward, 1538
  of liberty, 1072
  love of, 1011
  misunderstandings and, 1541
  moral obligation to, 1538–40
  patriotism and, 1019–20
  plagues of, 1382, 1393

preparations against invasion of, 1136

presence of God and, 211, 216–17

private, 767

of religion, 1489

of Roman Catholic Church, 1354

Romans and, 1203

separation from, 1381–85

sins of, 1382, 1393

of United States Constitution, 1501

weakness in government and, 1431

England. *See also* Bristol, England; Church of England; Great Britain; London, England; headings beginning with British; and specific kings

British Parliament and, 275, 282

Christian church and, 519

education in, 127

feudal system and, 1249

French Revolution and, 1246, 1355

Great Awakening in, xvii

Illuminati and, 1376

Jewish converts of, 1392

king as head of church government, 338

as part of Great Britain, 272

rule of, 126

taxation and, 283–84

Enthusiasm, 1243, 1245, 1254–61, 1287, 1298

Ephesus, 347

Ephraim, 41, 753, 754, 875, 1419, 1429

Ephraimites, 856

Epictetus, 1200*n*

Episcopal church

as denomination, 527

religious liberty and, 989

Smith's *Sermon Preached Before a Convention of the Episcopal Church*, 817–34

in southern colonies, 496

Epithets, 1544, 1546

Equality

American Revolution and, 1051, 1311

Christianity and, 1113

citizens' equal influence over free government, 1279, 1280

in education, 1073

gospel and, 1156, 1312

independence and, 1560

iniquity and, 1548

liberty and, 1064

men born equal, 637, 1312*n*

in property distribution, 1175

revenue laws and, 1178

right of, 56–57, 1121

Equity, 362, 366, 428, 1115

Error, human race and, 382

Erskine, 1376*n*

Esau, 379, 592, 725, 1497

Eskimaux, 1505, 1508

The Essential Rights and Liberties of Protestants (Williams), 53–118

Esther, 216, 590, 758

Eternity, 854, 862, 978. *See also* Immortality

Ethan the Ezrahite, 891

Ethiopia, 594, 1161*n*

Eugene IV, 1038, 1039

Euphrates River, 1368

Europe. *See also* French Revolution; and specific countries

African development and, 1049*n*

African slavery and, 1038, 1392

aristocracy in, 1288–89

atheism and, 1400

Europe, *continued*
  balance of power in, 1271
  colonial America and, 246, 504
  combined powers and, 1180, 1244,
    1246, 1285, 1355
  discovery and, 1038
  feudal system and, 1249, 1268, 1271
  forms of government and, 1497
  French domination of, 1247, 1347,
    1351, 1355
  George III and, 700–701
  governments of, 871
  Great Awakening in, xvii
  Great Britain's peace terms and,
    677
  history of, 1310–11
  knowledge and, 899
  liberty and, 1027, 1054, 1163
  Philip II and, 594
  political situation in, 1144, 1228,
    1299, 1311, 1335
  Protestantism in, 205
  religious liberty and, 783*n*
  revolutions and, 1313
  slavery and, 1203
  slave trade of, 1041*n*, 1047
  Stamp Act repeal and, 251
  tyranny and, 1226
  United States and, 654, 693,
    698–99, 799, 1232*n*, 1314
  war in, 1228
Eutaw, 781
Evander, 1205
Evangelism, xviii–xix, 1082. *See also*
  Great Awakening
Evans, Israel
  biographical information on, 1058
  *Sermon Delivered at the Annual
    Election*, 1059–78
Eve, 1051, 1457
Eve, George, 1080

Evils. *See also* Vice
  of absolute government, 1179
  American Revolution and, 856
  Canaan and, 932
  divine providence and, 620
  God and, 1534
  Griswold's *Overcoming Evil with
    Good*, 1531–54
  hearts of men and, 828
  liberty and, 1126
  love of importance, 1088
  political, 1193, 1194, 1252
  prevention of, 1441, 1444
  of private interests, 1010
  prosperity and, 839–53
  resistance to, 727, 853, 1388
  Smalley's *On the Evils of a Weak
    Government*, 1417–46
  turned into kindness, 219, 260
Executive branch. *See also* United
    States President
  Adams and, 1520
  balanced powers of, 802, 1176, 1343
  choice of officers, 1066
  justice and, 861
  religion and, 933
  virtue and, 933
Exousia, 444*n*
Ezra, 590

Fabii, 197
Fabius, 801
Factions. *See also* Political parties;
    Societies
  anarchy and, 1294
  choice of rulers and, 1426
  civil wars and, 1231, 1280, 1295
  connection with enemies and, 1384
  cruelty of, 1239
  dangers of, 1284, 1546
  forms of government and, 1264

free government and, 1270, 1271,
1278, 1279
French Revolution and, 1231, 1239,
1263, 1268–70, 1271–72, 1280, 1350
Genet and, 1229
Greece and, 1280
Israel's demand for king and, 1326
liberty and, 1267, 1278, 1294
magistrates and, 936
patriotism and, 850
political parties and, 928, 937, 960,
1227–28, 1271, 1273, 1534
reason and, 1071
Republican party and, 1547
Rome and, 1280, 1281–83
rulers and, 922, 927–28
savagery of, 1292–95
societies and, 1230–34, 1277–78
spirit of, 811–12
states and, 1227
true religion and, 1073
tyranny and, 1294
United States government and,
1228, 1232, 1294
Faith
Christian church and, 830
controversies in, 826, 829
human inventions and, 829
in Jesus Christ, 821–22
justification by faith alone, 410
love and, 827
pillars and, 16
pleasing God and, 33
points of, 829
scriptures as rule of faith and
practice, 62–64, 71–73, 75–76,
85–87, 94–98
service to God and, 1223
trial of, 827
without works, 833
Falmouth, 625n

Fanaticism and National
Convention of France, 1258,
1261–62
Fast-day sermons
Sewall's *Nineveh's Repentance and
Deliverance* as, 26–50
Sherman's *Scriptural Instructions to
Civil Rulers*, 375–407
as type of sermon, xxiii
Fasting
bodies and, 34
days of fasting proclamations, xxiii
divine judgments and, 33–36
of Nineveh, 30
prayer and, 35–36
repentance and, 36–40
royal proclamation for, 569
rulers and, 45–50
souls and, 34–35
war and, 563, 570, 572, 576–78
Fear of God
Chauncy's *Civil Magistrates Must
Be Just, Ruling in the Fear of God*,
139–77
children and, 961
civil society/civil union and, 916
duty to, 1320
government and, 916, 1446
judges and, 227
legislators and, 960
magistrates and, 139–77, 1069
man and, 1430
passions of men and, 1328
praise and, 982
rulers and, 166–68, 384–85, 392–95,
1328, 1469
Solomon and, 831–32
tyranny and, 167, 395
Washington and, 1409
Federal constitution. *See* United
States Constitution

Federal Convention of 1787, xvi, xxiv

Federal government. *See* United States government

The Federalist, xx

Federal party, 1522

Federalists, 1270, 1286, 1498, 1521, 1523, 1525

Felix, 125

Fenelon, 1014

Fenno, John, 1524, 1526–27*n*, 1527–28

Ferdinand (emperor), 747, 750

Ferne, Dr., 731

Feudal system, 950, 1248–49, 1250, 1268, 1271

Fielding, Henry, xvii

Fifth-day Lecture, xxiii

Filmer, 248

Fish, Joseph, 362*n*

Fishing, 462, 478, 513, 1225–26

Flanders, 1246

Fletcher, John
  Bible and the Sword, 561–78
  biographical information on, 560
  Wesley and, 412

Flood
  French Revolution compared to, 1393
  Jefferson and, 1454–59, 1462
  laws of nature and, 1502, 1504
  sin and, 332–33
  Voltaire and, 1503*n*
  woman and, 511–14

Foise, Earl of, 748

Fontenoy, battle of, 130

Forgiveness
  Christianity compared with philosophical religion, 1207, 1210
  of enemies, 585, 1543
  and Plato, 1202

Fornication, 1200–1201, 1200*n*

Fourth of July. *See also* Independence
  Dwight's *Duty of Americans at the Present Crisis*, 1365–94
  Emerson's *Oration in Commemoration of the Anniversary of American Independence*, 1557–69
  Hitchcock's *Oration in Commemoration of the Independence of the United States of America*, 1171–83
  Miller's *Sermon on the Anniversary of the Independence of America*, 1151–67
  political sermons and, xxiv

France. *See also* French Revolution; Paris; and other headings beginning with French
  John Adams and, 1523, 1527
  anarchy in, 1298, 1358, 1360
  antichristian empire and, 1393
  arbitrary government of, 424
  atheism in, 1252, 1253, 1262, 1265, 1266, 1268
  boasting of army, 547*n*
  Christian church and, 519
  civil wars and, 1299
  colonial America and, 198, 203, 240, 245, 246, 435
  colonial wars with, 477
  constitutions of, 1231, 1297
  despotism and, 1252, 1297, 1298
  dignity of man and, 907
  education in, 1251
  Federalists and, 1523
  Fenno and, 1524
  forms of government and, 1264, 1296
  free government and, 1180
  French Hugenots, 749

Great Britain and, 218, 597, 677, 700, 856

Illuminati and, 1375

independence of nations and, 1386

liberty and, 482, 997, 1027, 1071, 1076, 1299, 1497

Marius and, 1282*n*

Masons in, 1373

materialism and, 1253, 1259, 1265, 1348

National Assembly, 1239, 1352

National Convention of France, 1241–44, 1255, 1258, 1259–60, 1262–63

navy of, 697–98

persecution in, 1087

philosophers of, 1014

philosophists and, 1384

Protestantism in, 205, 515, 747, 750

Quebec and, 478

Roman Catholic Church and, 129, 135, 502, 502*n*, 515, 1371

slave trade of, 1041*n*, 1042–43, 1046

Spanish Armada and, 984

tyranny of, 1346

United States' alliance with, 650–51, 675, 693, 697, 699, 746–47, 780–81, 785–86, 801, 938, 1550

Francis I (king of France), 1240

Franklin, Benjamin
gratitude for, 1334
library of, 900
noble actions and, 893
peace negotiations and, 688
Price and, 1006
scientific research and, 897
William Smith and, 816
Webster and, 1236
Whitefield and, 120

Frassaniere, 747

Frederic II (king of Prussia), 1372, 1465

Frederick Palitine of the Rhine, 747

Fredericksburgh, Virginia, 1463*n*, 1471*n*

Free choice, xx, 382, 444

Freedom. *See also* Liberty; Rights
church-state relations and, 1118
of colonies, 637
education of youth and, 1073
of elections, 1065, 1467, 1471
French Revolution and, 1347
Glorious Revolution and, 870, 986
of Great Britain, 475
licentiousness and, 1036, 1440
martyrs of, 785
men born free, 637
perfect law of, xvi*n*
of the press, 986–87, 1347
prosperity and, 1061
religious, 1123
of sciences, 1181–82
temporary disorders and, 1178–79
of United States, 1061
of writing, 1251

Freedom of conscience. *See* Liberty of conscience

Freedom of worship. *See* Religious liberty

Free government. *See also* Democracy; Republican government
arts and sciences and, 1250
British constitution and, 424
checks on, 1422
citizens' equal influence over, 1279
defensive arms and, 1146
despotism compared with, 925, 1179
disorders of, 1178–79
factions and, 1270, 1271, 1278, 1279

Free government, *continued*
　France and, 1180
　magistrates compared with
　　despots, 925
　man's influence over, 900
　monarchy and, 1272
　morality and, 1410
　people's support of, 1143
　privileges of, 914
　sovereignty of the people and,
　　808
　United States government as
　　example of, 1126
　virtue and, 1333
Free-thinkers, 1108
French Academy, 1372
French and Indian Wars, 477–78, 816
French Dictionary of Arts and
　Sciences, 1372, 1372*n*
French Guinea Company, 1042
French Hugenots, 749, 1488
French Revolution
　agriculture and, 1239, 1248–49
　antichrist and, 1353, 1353*n*
　arts and, 1250–51
　atheism and, 1269, 1270, 1291, 1348
　causes of, 1240–47, 1269, 1374
　Christianity and, 1164–65*n*, 1266,
　　1270
　cruelties of, 1346–50, 1496
　democracy and, 1356
　domination and, 1355
　effects of, 1247–67, 1565–66
　Europe's combined powers and,
　　1180, 1244, 1246, 1285, 1355
　Europe's feudal system and, 1271
　excesses of, 1180–81
　executions of, 1265
　factions and, 1231, 1239, 1268–70,
　　1280, 1350
　feudal system and, 1268

　freedom of the press and, 1347
　French domination of Europe,
　　1247, 1347, 1351, 1355
　government and, 1266–67
　Griswold and, 1530
　Judaism and, 1350
　kings and, 1180
　laws and, 1265, 1297, 1298, 1347
　liberty and, 1163–64, 1179–80,
　　1268–70, 1357
　manufactures and, 1249–50, 1347
　millenium and, 1353*n*
　monarchy and, 1180, 1181, 1253, 1262,
　　1269, 1271, 1497
　morality and, 1239, 1264–66
　National Convention commis-
　　sioners and, 1241–44
　national debt and, 1247–48
　national treasury and, 1244–45
　passions of men and, 1297–98, 1358
　political parties and, 1239, 1266,
　　1269–70, 1272
　popes and, 1352–54
　religion and, 1251–64, 1266, 1347–48,
　　1351, 1358
　republican government and, 1271
　revenue sources and, 1247, 1347
　rights and, 1164*n*, 1179, 1269
　Roman Catholic Church and,
　　1244–45, 1251, 1269, 1348–50,
　　1358–59
　sciences and, 1250–51
　slavery as tyranny and, 1347, 1352
　Tappan and, 1102
　trade and commerce and, 1239,
　　1250, 1347, 1356
　treason and, 1270
　United States and, 1271, 1285,
　　1355–58, 1566
　United States government and,
　　1356, 1357*n*

Webster's *Revolution in France,*
    1237–99
West Indies and, 1350–51
Frugality, 556–57, 876, 938, 965
Fuillans, 1253, 1272, 1281, 1286, 1295–96
Fundy, Bay of, 477

Gabriel, 189
Gad, 635, 636, 760
Gage, Thomas, 312, 482, 512, 692, 756
Galatians, 1033, 1062
Galileo, 1182, 1506–7
Gallatin, Albert, 1478, 1511, 1522*n*
Gamaliel, 1593
Gardiner, Colonel, 132
Garrier, 1295
Gaspee affair, 302, 306, 309–11
Gates, Horatio, 625*n*
Gath, 799, 1402
Gee, Mr., 752
Genet, Citizen, 1229, 1498
Geneva, 1352, 1357, 1385, 1393
Genghis Khan, 1247
Genoa
    antichristian empire and, 1371, 1393
    Berenger and, 640
    civil union and, 1385
    connection with enemies and, 1384
    French Revolution and, 1352, 1357
    slave trade and, 1042
Genseric (king of the Vandals), 1247
George I (king of England), 596
George II (king of England), 124–26,
    596
George III (king of England)
    *Dialogue Between the Devil, and
    George III, Tyrant of Britain,*
    689–710

Gage and, 756
North and, 720, 758
prayer resistance and, 767
privy council of, 705
reign of, 688
repentance of, 725
rights of prescription and, 1563
swearing and, 695–96, 703
as tyrant, 689–710, 730
Georgia
    American Revolution battles of,
        781
    Holcombe's *Sermon Occasioned by
        the Death of Washington,*
        1397–1414
    population breakdown of, 1046*n*
    Wesley and, 410
    Zubly's *Humble Enquiry into the
        Nature of the Dependency of the
        American Colonies upon the
        Parliament of Great Britain,*
        267–99
Germaine, 694, 698, 704, 706–7
Germans and French and Indian
    War, 816
Germany
    adulation and, 1018
    anabaptists of, 1083
    antichristian empire and, 1371, 1393
    Christians' use of defensive arms,
        748–49
    feudal system and, 1249
    heathens converted, 1392
    Illuminati and, 1375
    Luther and, 83
    Masons in, 1373
    mercenaries from Germany, 641
    Protestants of, 750
    Reformation and, 543
Gerry, Elbridge, 1340
Geshem the Arabian, 757

Gibbon, Edward, 1465, 1492
Gibeah, 570–71, 593, 953
Gibeon, 904, 1399
Gibeonites, 788, 1050
Gibraltar, 272, 284
Gideon, 594, 752–53, 953, 954, 1403
Gifford, 1376n
Gilboa, 1403, 1414n
Gileadites, 953
Ginavel, Captain, 748
Girondists, 1263
Glocester, Virginia, 781
Glorious Revolution
    century sermons on, xxiii, 970,
        971–1000
    conscience and, 1020
    defensive arms and, 719
    divine providence and, 985
    freedom and, 870
    gratitude for, 1020–21, 1024
    history of, 995
    James II and, 1021
    liberty and, 476, 985–88
    Price's *Discourse on the Love of Our
        Country*, 1005–28
    principles of, 639, 1021, 1024
    property and, 986, 1020
    Winchester's *Century Sermon on the
        Glorious Revolution*, 971–1000
Goango, 1041
God. *See also* Cause of God; Divine
    judgments; Divine providence;
    Fear of God; Gratitude to God;
    Holy Spirit; Jesus Christ; Laws
    of God
    Aaron as minister of, 342–43
    American Revolution and,
        522–23n, 549, 618, 720, 798–801
    anger of, 403, 613–14

attributes of, 978–82, 1000, 1222,
    1584
authority of, 382, 1191
belief in, 611
benevolence of, 1013
care of man and, 889–90
Christian church's protection by,
    522–24
Christianity's teaching of, 1113
colonial America's successes and,
    625, 787, 800
colonial militia and, 623–24, 717–18
conscience and, 225, 1062, 1064,
    1068, 1085, 1467
covenant with, 220–22
death and, 1403
defensive arms and, 721–22, 736,
    738–39, 759–66
deliverances of, 398–407, 1222
dependency of all creatures on,
    793–94, 879
dispensations of, 11–12, 18
Dunbar's *Presence of God with His
    People*, 209–30
duty to, 223, 239, 557, 584, 1093
enemies of, 1379–80
evil and, 1534
false prophets and, 1369
fighting for Israel and, 976, 977
as first cause, 797, 798
forsaking God, 224, 226–27, 229–30
free agency as gift of, 444
freedom of choice and, 810
government and, 18, 19, 20–21,
    143–44, 394, 453–54, 486,
    738–39, 780, 794, 795, 946, 1037
government not of, 735–36
government of, 382, 611, 661, 1192,
    1207, 1207–9, 1315
guidance of, 794, 926
hand of God and, 784–85,
    798–801, 840, 983–84

happiness and, 1189, 1209, 1211, 1215, 1315

human nature as image of, 1077

Illuminati and, 1374

Indians and, 893–94

instruments of, 798

Israel and, 218, 219, 230, 590, 786, 787, 856, 1462

jealousy of, 1393–94

as Jehovah, 590, 604, 913, 917–18, 948, 954, 955, 978, 980, 981, 1105, 1582–83

Jews and, 124, 595, 618–20, 631, 759, 795, 854, 1189

Keteltas's *God Arising and Pleading His People's Cause*, 581–605

kings and, 316, 664, 767

love of man, 1316–17

love of righteousness, 860–61

man as image of, 887–88, 896

man's accountability to, 1191, 1192

mercy of, 621–23, 631, 1539

military forces and, 213, 214, 227, 1147

moral perfections of, 888, 1193–94, 1207, 1208, 1209, 1211

nations' destruction and, 796, 1335

nations under gospel and, 854

natural rights and, 444–45

obedience of man and, xx, 585

obligations to, 878–79

omnipotent spirit of, 591–93, 662, 862, 979, 1013, 1315, 1319

omnipresence of, 979, 1328

omniscience of, 978–79, 1191, 1319, 1338

pillar of earth belonging to, 17–19

power of, 18, 382, 620, 662–63, 922

praise of, 794, 981–82

presence of, 211–30, 624

pride and, 1445

prophets and, 212

public affairs and, 780

public injustice and, 847

reliance on, 1391

religion as voluntary obedience to, 347

religious establishments and, 991

repentance and, 31–32, 38–42, 523, 619, 795

respect for rulers and, 922

righteousness of, 1013

righteousness of nations and, 678–79

rulers' accountability to, 1112, 1121

rulers as ministers of, 806, 922, 1019, 1070, 1422, 1433, 1469

safety and, 214–20, 1379

service of, 906, 1223

sin and, 42, 661

as sovereign of world, 611–12, 786–87, 794, 795, 796–804, 810–12

subjection and, 724

submission to, 143–44, 382, 554

as superintendent over worldly affairs, 793–94, 1221, 1315

as trinity, 1583

true religion, 1073

trust in, 549, 583, 1223

truth and, 1090

tyranny and, 599

United States and, 782, 783, 783*n*, 786–87

United States Constitution and, 1471–72

vengeance for enemies of his people, 617–18, 621, 1393

victory and, 801

virtue and, 873–74, 1317, 1318

war and, 570, 571, 1137–38, 1376

Washington's greatness and, 1399

will of, 143–44, 382, 541, 738–39, 828, 1037, 1315, 1326

wisdom of, 674–75

God, *continued*
  word of, 589–91
  works of, 1221
  worship and, 1126
  wrath of, 1051
  wrath of men and, 662, 1180
God Arising and Pleading His People's
  Cause (Keteltas), 581–605
Gods of paganism, 1195
Gog, 860
Golden rule, 1185
Gold mines of Brazil, 1041
Goliath, 548, 754–55, 799, 1315
Gomorrha, 593, 804, 842
Good Hope, Cape of, 1040
Goodrich, Elizur
  biographical information on, 910
  Principles of Civil Union and
    Happiness Considered and
    Recommended, 911–40
Gordian, 1205
Gordon, William, xv
Gospel. *See also* Jesus Christ;
    Scriptures
  abolition and, 1203
  blessings of, 863
  civil society/civil union and,
    923–24
  commands of, 957
  doctrines of, 1062, 1063
  duty to support, 1092–93
  equality and, 1156
  God of, 1189
  God's conduct toward nations, 854
  gospel-privileges, 872
  history of, 993
  indifference to, 881
  Israel's worship and, 949
  knowledge of, 1091, 1438, 1580
  laws and, 1094–95

  liberty and, 1062
  motives to virtue and, 1194
  newness in, 820n
  oppression and, 1310
  policy of, 1535
  politics and, 1452
  preaching of, 893, 934
  religion of, 824
  restraint from vice and, 1194
  rulers and, 1157
  salvation and, 923–24
  study of, 935
  success of, 822, 879
  teachings of, 826
  temperance and, 1159
  toleration and, 1515
  truths of, 1070, 1090, 1575
  weakness in government and, 1431
  worship and, 1062
Goths, 1258, 1270, 1510, 1567
Government. *See also* Church-state
    relations; Constitutions; Free
    government; Governments,
    forms of; Religious establish-
    ments; Republican government;
    Tyranny; United States govern-
    ment; and specific types of
    government
  administration of, 387, 646, 876–77
  altering of, 1085
  appointment of, 168–71
  authority of, 20, 285–86
  balance of powers in, 302, 487,
    1176–77, 1343–44
  benevolent design of, 805
  as blessing, 936, 1317
  Christianity's influence on, 1155
  civil society/civil union and, 1268,
    1298, 1385–86
  coercive law and, xx
  colleges and, 163

Colman's *Government as Pillar of the Earth*, 9–24
of colonial America, 240, 490–91
compact and, 1083–84
consent and, 492, 634–35, 1062, 1066
corruption in, 960, 1024
defensive arms and, 1141–43
dependent governments, 147, 150
design of, 739–40, 1142
dissolution of, 383
distrust of, 848, 875
ecclesiastical government contrasted with, 335–39
ecclesiastical government in conflict with, 102–5, 339–48
education and, 163, 169, 366n, 808–9, 905, 1073, 1331
in Europe, 871
executive power of, 336–37
families and, 1325
fear of God and, 916, 1446
formation of, 453
framing of, 1021, 1068
free choice and, 382, 642
French Revolution and, 1266–67
fundamental laws and, 918
God and, 18, 19, 20–21, 143–44, 394, 453–54, 486, 738–39, 780, 794, 795, 946, 1037
government not of God, 735–36
government of God, 382, 611, 661, 1192, 1207, 1207–9, 1315
gratitude for, 934, 1183
honoring engagements and promises, 649–50
Illuminati and, 1374
independence and, 490
inequality in, 875
innovations in, 1564–65
of Israel, 402–3, 634, 945–47, 952–53, 957, 1325–26, 1419

Jesus Christ as foundation of, 15
judges and, 337
justice and, 1066
knowledge and, 1013, 1410
laws of God and, 916
legislative authority of, 387
liberty and, xxiv, 58–59, 263–64, 331–35, 382, 596, 1037, 1142, 1155
Masons and, 1373
Moses Mather on, 486–88
natural aristocracy and, 920–21
necessity of, 486, 812, 876
obedience to, 80, 740–41, 877
oppression and, 735, 1427–30
order and, 13, 18, 142–43, 378
origin of, 56–58, 486–88
parenthood and, 445n
passions of men and, 1325, 1333
peace and, 1142
philosophers and, 1133
as pillars of earth, 13–17, 19–20
political parties and, 1298
power of, 58, 59, 79–80, 321, 339, 356, 456, 1515
presence of God and, 223, 225
principles of, xvi, 1083–84, 1133
private character and, 917, 1121, 1378
property and, 58–59, 60
prosperity and, 1142
public debt and, 154–56
public expenses of, 938, 1433–34, 1437, 1521
public faith in, 646–47, 650, 653, 809–10, 847, 860, 938
punishment and, 59–60
Puritans and, 96
purpose of, 58–59, 83, 1016
qualifications of, 919–21
reason and, 143–45, 1176
resistance to, 735–36, 738–39, 872
restraint in, 991
revolutions and, 1296

Government, *continued*
  right of private judgment and,
    97–99
  rights and, 445–51
  rules of, 738–39
  safety and, 143, 739–40, 1176
  salaries of, 401–2*n*
  schemes for, 404–6
  scriptures and, 76–77, 375–407,
    1431–33
  secrets of, 770
  security and, 1142
  Sherman's *Scriptural Instructions to
    Civil Rulers*, 375–407
  slavery compared with, 427–29,
    488
  Smalley's *On the Evils of a Weak
    Government*, 1417–46
  sovereignty of the people and,
    959
  stability of, 918, 927
  of states, 1231–32
  submission to, 332, 334, 1126,
    1433–34
  suitability of, 454
  support of, 1146
  violence and, 1066
  virtue and, 1335
  war preparations during peace
    and, 1134
  Washington and, 1405
  weakness of, 1422–25
Government the Pillar of the Earth
  (Colman), 9–24
Governments, forms of. *See also* specific types of government, such
  as Anarchy; Absolute government; Republican government
  American manners and, 1561
  appropriateness of, 1037
  civil society/civil union and, 382
  conflict between, 1497

  factions and, 1264
  France and, 1296
  origins of, 870–71
  scriptures and, 1326–27
  sovereignty of the people and,
    486–87
  spectrum of, 1176–77
  submission and, 1434–35
  United States government and,
    1526
  Washington and, 1405
  weakness and, 1421
Grace
  Dunbar and, 208
  Jesus Christ's victories of, 200
  Jews and, 854
  kingdom of Jesus Christ and, 190
  religious test and, 1083
  resistance to tyrants and, 734–35
  signs of, 826
  works and, 833
Grafton, Augustus Henry, 3rd Duke
  of Grafton, 323
Grants from British Crown, 457
Gratitude. *See also* Gratitude to God
  alliances and, 1229
  duty of, 1343
  for Glorious Revolution, 1024
  for government, 934, 1183
  ingratitude, 844–45
  to king, 223
  for liberty, 1074
  for rulers, 1334
  for United States government,
    1227, 1343
  Washington and, 1290
Gratitude to God. *See also*
  Thanksgiving-day sermons
  benevolence and, 879
  for divine providence, 1316
  for Glorious Revolution, 1020–21

history and, 1309
for liberty in United States,
    1076–77
national prosperity and, 840, 843
for peace, 775, 1346, 1358
political parties and, 1535
public prosperity and, 1226
rulers and, 223
for United States Constitution,
    1165–66
for United States government,
    1343–46
Great Awakening, xiii, xvii, 8, 52, 120,
    208, 658. *See also* Evangelism;
    Second Awakening
Great Britain. *See also* American
    Revolution; Church of
    England; Colonial America;
    England; Glorious Revolution;
    Taxation; Taxation of colonial
    America; and headings begin-
    ning with British and specific
    kings
advantages from colonial America,
    477–79
Africa and, 567
blessings of, 996
cause of God and, 596
choice of ministers and, 115–17
church-state relations and, 990
colonial militia and, 1140
colonial sympathizers in, 256–57,
    517, 640–42, 799
credit of, 649–50
dependent governments and, 147,
    272, 277–82, 286, 290, 295
dignity of man and, 907
enemies of, 135, 477
Federalists and, 1523
Fenno and, 1524, 1527
France and, 218, 597, 677, 700, 856
freedom of, 475

freedom of speech and, 60
freedom of the press and, 987
God's defense of, 218
God's help to United States and,
    787
gun-powder plot, 216
heathens and, 1050
Ireland and, 253
Irish Catholics and, 1359, 1360
Jews as citizens of, 1023
Jews compared to, 124–25
jurisdiction of, 455–56
justification for war, 571–72
knowledge and, 899
laws of, 276, 308, 309, 950–51
liberty and, 306, 320, 402, 596–97,
    602–3, 639, 970, 1027, 1313
mercies and duties of, 123–36
national debt of, 649, 777, 809, 847,
    847*n*, 1026
patriotism and, 1026
peace terms of, 676–77, 688, 708
Philip II and, 982
philosophers of, 1014
power of wrath, 675
property infringements of, 640
redress of grievances and, 675–76
Reformation and, 543
religious liberty and, 988
rights of, 307, 415
Roman Catholic Church and, 503
slavery as tyranny and, 240, 986,
    994, 1027
slavery of Negroes, 567, 641
slave trade of, 1041*n*, 1042–43, 1046
Spain and, 543, 597, 982–85, 1042
Spanish Armada and, 983–85
spies of, 1526*n*
Stamp Acts and, 238–39
territories of, 272
trade and commerce of, 240, 242,
    1521

Great Britain, *continued*
    treaties with United States, 1521
    tyranny and, 694, 720, 730
    United States' relationship with,
        999, 1141, 1550
    Whitefield's *Britain's Mercies and
        Britain's Duties*, 121–36
    Zubly's *Humble Enquiry into the
        Nature of the Dependency of the
        American Colonies upon the
        Parliament of Great Britain*,
        267–99
Greaves, 698
Greece. *See also* Athens; Sparta
    Anaxagoras and, 1182
    Arabians and, 1050
    Delphic oracles of, 1256–57
    education and, 1204, 1442
    factions and, 1280
    Goths and, 1567
    greatness of, 1552
    justice and, 1202
    knowledge and, 899
    learning and, 900
    liberty and, 1016, 1160n
    man's noble actions and, 892
    monarchy of, 193
    Olympic games and, 1259
    patriotism and, 850
    Philip and, 1526
    philosophers of, 1255, 1261–62, 1270
    public virtue and, 805
    as republican government, 1231
    slavery and, 245, 1049, 1076, 1201
    tyranny and, 761
    vice and, 1197, 1199–1206
Greene, L. F., 1080
Greenland, 1505
Gregory I, 1162n
Grenada, 1043n
Grieve, A. J., 1006

Grimstone, Sir Harbottle, 96
Griswold, Stanley
    biographical information on, 1530
    Overcoming Evil with Good, 1531–54
Grotius, Hugo, 712, 1493
Grotius de jure Belli, 731, 732
Guadaloupe, 1043n
Guernsey, 272, 276, 282, 284, 289
Gugorious, 746
Guienne, 748
Guillotine, 1242–43, 1245, 1248, 1263,
    1295, 1346, 1376
Guinea, 1038, 1040, 1043, 1047
Guise, duke of, 1293
Gun-powder plot, 216
Gustavas Adolphus, 750
Habeas corpus act, 450
Haerlem, 749
Hagar, 1033
Haggai, 757
Hainault, 749
Ham, 19, 974, 1118, 1195, 1510
Haman, 216–17, 541, 616–17, 665, 758,
    1334
Hamilton, Alexander
    adultery and, 1499n, 1511
    Federalists and, 1523
    France and, 1340
    T. Pinckney and, 1522
    talents of, 1522n
    United States Constitution and,
        1524, 1527
Hammond, 1498
Hampden, Mr., 544
Hancock, John, 494, 608, 702, 1102,
    1340
Hannah, 11
Hannibal, 1086

Hanover, 454

Hanover family, 396, 438, 596, 988

Happiness
arts and sciences and, 1071
atheism and, 1462
Christianity and, 1124
civil society/civil union and, 915, 932, 1157
education and, 1268
elections and, 1070
enemies' capacity for, 1539
foundations for, 855
God and, 1189, 1209, 1211, 1215, 1315
Goodrich's *Principles of Civil Union and Happiness Considered and Recommended*, 911–40
Illuminati and, 1374
industry and, 876
infidelity and, 1192, 1209, 1210
laws and, 1065–66
laws of God and, 914
liberty and, 1061
man's capacity for, 892
misery and, 857
morality and, 1105
national, 873–78, 1153
obedience to laws and, 1067
of people, 1067
piety and, 1211
political parties and, 1274
of posterity, 878
presence of God and, 214–20
public administration and, 919–21
religion and, 1107–11
repentance and, 881
republican government and, 1319
rights and, 1068
scriptures and, 1325
security of, 840–41
virtue and, 873–78, 1211, 1318

Harbor closures, 399, 481, 513

Hargrove, John
biographical information on, 1572
Sermon on the Second Coming of Christ, 1573–96

Hartford, Connecticut
Edwards's *Necessity of the Belief of Christianity*, 1187–1216
Goodrich's *Principles of Civil Union and Happiness Considered and Recommended*, 911–40
Griswold's *Overcoming Evil with Good*, 1531–54
Smalley's *On the Evils of a Weak Government*, 1417–46
Wales's *Dangers of Our National Prosperity; and the Way to Avoid Them*, 837–63

Hartley, Mr., 641, 1493

Harvey, Nathaniel, 355

Hastings, 1047

Havanna, 478

Hayners, 1546

Hazael, 1333

Health, 1224–25

Hearts of men
belonging to Jesus Christ and, 821
evil and, 828
God's hands and, 797–98
heathens and, 823
Jesus Christ in, 834
Jesus Christ's kingdom and, 822
love and, 827–28
perverseness of temper in, 822
social conduct and, 875

Heathens. *See also* Idolatry; Indians; Pagans and paganism
Christians and, 1051
conversion of, 1392
death and, 1404

Heathens, *continued*
  dependence on supreme power, 794
  as dissenters, 1092, 1095
  divine providence and, 1221
  humanity of, 1202–6
  idolatry and, 823, 980
  immortality of soul and, 888, 1400
  persecutions and, 745–47, 1197–99
  philosophers, 854
  philosophy of, 1438
  religious liberty and, 1034
  Roman Catholic Church and, 1050
  truth and, 1090
  vice and, 1199–1206
  worship of, 1197
Hebron, 1402
Heimert, Alan, xvii
Helots, 1203
Helvetia, 20, 748
Helvetius, 1289
Heman, 891
Henry, 988
Henry, Patrick, 374
Henry, prince of Portugal, 1038, 1039
Henry III (king of England), 447
Henry IV (emperor of Rome), 716
Henry IV (king of England), 447
Henry IV (king of France), 997, 1261
Henry VII (king of England), 454
Henry VIII (king of England), 74, 83, 95, 134, 502–3, 526
Herbert, George, 1465
Herbois, Collot D., 1384
Hercules, 1257
Heresies, 204, 1088, 1263, 1514
Hermogenes, Captain, 746
Herod, 188

Hesse, 701, 781
Hezekiah, 16, 316, 534, 722, 841, 1379, 1420
Highlander uprising, 530
Hillsborough, Lord, 323
Hind Let Loose, A (Shields), 712
Hindus, 1286
History
  of American Revolution, 719–20, 1173–74
  of Bible, 1133
  causes of French Revolution and, 1240
  of Christianity, 993–94
  church-state relations and, 1117–19
  of civil wars, 1292
  divine providence and, 544, 1309, 1312, 1314, 1392
  education and, 957
  of Europe, 1310–11
  gratitude to God and, 1309
  of Jacobin Society, 1376*n*
  knowledge of military forces and, 1140
  liberty and, 1016, 1075–76
  Mosaic, 1457
  objects of worship and, 1256
  of slave trade, 1038–47
  tyranny and, 1075–76
  vice and, 1199
  William III and, 994
Hitchcock, Enos
  biographical information on, 1170, 1172
  Oration in Commemoration of the Independence of the United States of America, 1171–83
Hoadley, 258
Hoadly, Benjamin, Bishop, 1014
Hobbes, Thomas, 1465, 1492

Hodge, George, 1150

Hogarth, William, xvii

Holcombe, Henry
  biographical information on, 1396
  Sermon Occasioned by the Death of Washington, xxiv, 1397–1414

Holidays and French Revolution, 1259

Holiness, 891–92, 981. *See also* Piety; Virtue

Holyrood House, 127

Holy Spirit
  civil and ecclesiastical government, 337
  covenant of circumcision and, 340
  gentiles and, 1034
  inspiration of, 591
  pentecost and, 1588
  piety and, 855
  prayer and, 35
  redemption and, 1055
  repentance and, 45
  Roman Catholic Church and, 1354*n*
  sermons and, xxi
  subjection to tyranny, 759
  trinity and, 1583

Home, Henry (Lord Kames), 1458, 1458*n*, 1505

Homer, 898, 1200

Honesty. *See* Truth

Honor
  of children to parents, 1432
  for dead, 1403
  elections and, 1065
  king and, 251–52, 1019
  as motive to virtue, 1192–93
  personal dignity and, 1193
  public order and, 1109

temptations of, 859
  virtue and, 1189

Honorius, 1206

Hooker, Thomas, 1546

Hopkins, Samuel, 440, 884, 1030

Horace, 837

Hortensius, 1201*n*

Hosea, 37

Hottentots, 1508

House of Commons. *See* British House of Commons

House of Lords. *See* British House of Lords

House of Representatives, 277, 280, 803, 1553. *See also* Continental Congress; United States Congress

Howe, Charles, 574, 692

Humane Society, 1130

Humanity of heathens, 1202–6

An Humble Enquiry into the Nature of the Dependency of the American Colonies upon the Parliament of Great Britain (Zubly), 267–99, 422

Hume, David
  argument of infidels and, 1492
  Christianity in colonial America and, 1380
  as enemy of Christ, 1161*n*, 1465
  God's mixed character and, 1207
  mind of man and, 1254, 1255
  Price and, 1006

Humility
  Thayer's *Discourse Delivered at the Roman Catholic Church in Boston*, 1341–61
  Washington and, 1408

Hungarians, 749

Hungerford, Mr., 276

Huntington, Samuel, 910, 924, 1187, 1551

Huram, 16

Hus, John, 204

Hussites, 1263

Hutcheson, Francis, 1006

Hutchinson, Thomas, 482, 512

Hypocrisy, 347, 1468–69, 1484, 1490, 1519*n*

Iceland, 1505

Idolatry. *See also* Pagans and
    paganism
  adulation and, 1018
  corruption and, 822–23
  as crime, 948
  defensive arms and, 763
  divine providence and, 1221
  enthusiasm and, 1255
  God compared with, 980–81
  Judaism and, 946, 949, 954, 955,
    1062
  reason and, 1286
  superstition and, 1034, 1062, 1255

Illuminati, 1355*n*, 1374–76, 1380, 1383

Immortality
  of enemies, 1539
  future state of existence and,
    1192–94, 1207, 1209–10
  heathens and, 888, 1400
  Jesus Christ and, 1318–19
  scriptures and, 1325
  of soul, 888–89

Inanimate world, 192

Independence. *See also* American
    Revolution; Declaration of
    Independence
  charters and charter rights and,
    870

  of colonies from each other, 491
  decision for, xvi, 291, 638, 641, 642,
    646
  divine providence and, 639, 699,
    958
  Dwight's *Duty of Americans, at the
    Present Crisis*, 1365–94
  Emerson's *Oration in
    Commemoration of the Anniversary
    of American Independence*,
    1557–69
  France's destruction of, 1386
  Great Britain's oppression as
    cause of, 638, 670–72, 701
  Hitchcock's *Oration in
    Commemoration of the
    Independence of the United States
    of America*, 1171–83
  liberty and, 1061
  Moses Mather on, 488–92
  Miller's *Sermon on the Anniversary of
    the Independence of America*, 1151–67
  obedience to British laws and, 271,
    281
  as peace condition, 707
  price of, 860, 876
  religious liberty and, 417–18
  retrospective on, 1153–54
  status among nations and, 638–39
  taxation and, 277, 296, 419
  trade and commerce and, 638, 1560

India, 272, 284, 1038

Indians
  British army and navy and, 625,
    625*n*, 641
  colonial America and, 240, 245,
    310, 455
  conquest and, 1010
  discovery of America and, 454
  as enemies, 1175
  God and, 893–94
  as inhabitant of America, 1309

instigations of, 599, 701
knowledge and, 899
laws of Great Britain and, 309
Mohican Indians, 1186
natural aristocracy and, 1289
as original proprietors of
    America, 456
persecution and, 1198
Quebec bill and, 514
rebellion and, 309
reduction of, 477
siding with British, 781
treatment of captives, 1203
vice and, 1196
wars with, 477, 1230, 1232*n*
Indigo production, 1041*n*
Industry
of colonial America, 241
feudal system and, 1249
fruits of, 1175
happiness and, 876
as moral duty, 556, 965
necessity of, 869
paper money and, 938
property and, 1178
spirit of, 939
Infant baptism, 339–40, 344, 347, 361
Infidelity
arguments of, 1492–93
atheism and, 1464
Bible interpretation and, 1091
Christianity and, 14, 69, 990,
    1192–93, 1474
church-state relations and, 1494
civil rulers and, 1469–71
connection with enemies and, 1384
dignity of man and, 894, 895
future state of existence and,
    1192–94, 1209
happiness and, 1192, 1209, 1210
hypocrisy and, 1468–69

increase of, 1472–73
Jefferson and, 1451–76, 1499, 1501–18
liberty and, 1036
liberty of conscience and, 1465–68
licentiousness and, 1464
Mazzei and, 1463
moral government of God and,
    1192, 1207–8
Mosaic history and, 1457
nature and, 1192
origin of mankind and, 1459
pardon and, 1210
persecutions and, 1489
philosophy and, 1566
as political evil, 1194
punishment and, 1194
reason and, 1209
religious establishment and, 1088
revolutions and, 1432
Sabbath and, 1470–71
scriptures and, 1453–54
second advent and, 1591
toleration and, 1490, 1493
United States and, 1438
United States President and, 1468,
    1474, 1476
youth and, 1472
Influence
aristocracy and, 1289–91
of British Crown, 436
of Christianity on government,
    1155
equal influence over free govern-
    ment, 900, 1279, 1280
French Republican party's influ-
    ence over people, 1243, 1292
governmental influence on peti-
    tions, 871
of irreligion, 1213–14
of ministers, 1481
personal influence, 1289–91
of religion, 1110–11, 1317–18

Influence, *continued*
  of societies, 1279, 1289, 1291
  of vice, 1213–14
  of Washington, 1289–90
Ingratitude, 844
Iniquity, 1548
Innocent VIII, 747
Inquisition
  Court of, 96
  Portugal and, 1263
  Protestants and, 502*n*
  public good and, 1527
  Roman Catholic Church and, 1488
  Spain and, 997, 1263, 1522*n*
  unjust nature of, 388
Invasions. *See also* Defense and
    defensive arms
  government and, 870
  internal peace and, 874
  preparations against, 1135, 1136,
    1139–41, 1145, 1147
  of rights and property, 923
  United States government and,
    1227
Ireland. *See also* Great Britain
  antichristian empire and, 1393
  British Parliament and, 275–76,
    282, 464
  civil office eligibility and, 1023
  constitution of, 273
  dependency of, 278–80
  Great Britain and, 253, 272, 397*n*
  Protestant charity schools of, 127
  rights of, 654
  rule of, 126
  Spanish Armada and, 985
  taxation and, 284, 289–90, 418
Irish Catholics, 1359, 1360

Irreligion. *See also* Infidelity
  connection with enemies and, 1384
  divine providence and, 1309
  influence of, 1213–14
  Jeremiah and, 1444
  luxury and, 1337
  prevalence of, 1445
  United States Constitution and,
    1471–72
  vice and, 1111
  virtue and, 1320
  Voltaire and, 1372
Isaac, 592, 593, 1033, 1500, 1581
Isaiah
  dignity of man and, 887
  God as savior, 618
  God as sovereign and, 796
  Jesus Christ and, 187, 1583
  justice and, 837
  kings and, 1420
  Roman Catholic Church and, 499
  war and, 573
  Zion and, 586
Ishmael, 1033, 1050
Isis, 1256
Island of Man, 272, 276
Israel. *See also* Jerusalem; Jews; Judah;
    Judaism
  Abimelech and, 753
  Ahaz as ruler of, 315
  Americans compared to, 631
  Ammon and, 753–54
  Balaam and, 216
  Benjamin and, 763
  blasphemers and, 345
  constitution of, 636–37, 645
  David as ruler of, 144, 187, 316,
    383–84
  defensive arms as duty and, 760,
    761–62, 763
  divine providence and, 593–94

elders of, 779
electors of, 920–21
factions and, 928
forty years in wilderness, 776
gentiles and, 612
God and, 218, 219, 230, 590, 856
government of, 402–3, 634, 779,
    945–46, 952–53, 957, 1325–26,
    1419
Jerusalem and, 913
Joab and, 553
judges era of, 952–55
kings era of, 955–56, 1547
lack of respect for, 951
laws of, 945, 947–48, 1329
Midianites and, 763
military forces of, 946, 953–54
mourning and, 1402
oppression of, 631, 1419
Pharaoh and, 777, 973, 974, 1476
progress of, 950, 951
property and, 1175
prosperity and, 839, 946, 952, 1335
rebellion of, 722
reputation of, 951, 957
restoration of, 784
road to Canaan and, 476
senate of, 946, 952, 955
sons of Belial and, 570–71
tribes of, 929, 946–47, 952, 954,
    955, 999–1000
weaknesses of, 952
worship of, 335, 946, 948–49
Issachar, 378, 758–59
Italy
    Christian church and, 519
    feudal system and, 1249
    French Revolution and, 1246, 1247,
        1390
    Illuminati and, 1375
    Marius and, 1282
        Mazzei and, 1513n
        pope and, 997
        religion and, 1252
        Roman Catholic Church and, 1371
        Spanish Armada and, 983
        Sulla and, 1283
Ithuriel, 1492

Jabin (king of Canaan), 751
Jacksonian Democrats, 1080
Jacob
    defensive arms as duty and,
        758–59, 760
    divine providence and, 593
    Egypt and, 973
    Esau and, 592
    Laban and, 590
    prayer and, 35
    tents of, 776
Jacobin Society. See also French
    Revolution
    American Revolution compared
        with, 1284–85
    anarchy and, 1358
    bigotry and, 1254, 1257, 1264
    Christianity and, 1239, 1253, 1257
    cockade of liberty and, 1261
    factions and, 1263, 1271–72
    Festival of Reason and, 1286–88
    French Revolution causes and,
        1241, 1269
    Fuillans and, 1286, 1295–96
    heresies and, 1263
    history of, 1376n
    monarchy and, 1262, 1287
    National Convention commis-
        sioners and, 1241–42
    obedience and, 1360–61
    Osgood and, 1218
    passions of men and, 1285–86
    pope and, 1353

Jacobin Society, *continued*
  religion and, 1291
  savagery of, 1292–95
  Sulla and Marius compared to,
    1281, 1283
  tactics of, 1291–92
  treason and, 1293–97
  in United States, 1292
  Wortman and, 1525
Jacobites, 296, 530
Jahiers, Captain, 748
Jairus, 78
Jamaica, 1042, 1043, 1043*n*, 1044,
    1044–45*n*
James, Saint, 14, 309, 695
James I (king of England), 96, 454,
    462, 747, 750
James II (king of England)
  charters and, 870
  civil liberties and, 157
  controversy of, 397*n*
  Glorious Revolution and, 1021
  liberty and, 320–21, 596, 603
  popish plot and, 126, 134
  tyranny and, 395–96
Japhet, 1510
Jay, John, 688, 1334
Jefferies, 1486*n*
Jefferson, Thomas
  atheism and, 1461–62, 1467, 1470,
    1517*n*
  Backus and, 328
  Bible and, 1456*n*
  character of, 1499, 1512–14, 1552
  Chauncy and, 790
  chosen people of God and, 1460,
    1460–61*n*, 1462
  Christianity and, 1454, 1460, 1464,
    1465, 1473, 1483, 1499
  conduct of, 1464, 1552–53
    conscience of, 1467–68
    days of prayer, fasting, and
      thanksgiving proclamations,
      xxiii–xxiv
    Deism and, 1473, 1483, 1495, 1499,
      1500–1501, 1517
    elections and, 1483, 1494, 1498–1500,
      1526, 1527
    flood and, 1454–59, 1462, 1501–4
    Griswold and, 1530
    inaugural speech of, 1553*n*
    as infidel, 1451–76, 1499, 1501–18
    liberty of conscience and, 1516
    Bishop James Madison and, 1306
    Mason and, 1448
    Mason's *Voice of Warning to
      Christians*, 1449–76
    Negroes as inferior and, 1457–59,
      1502, 1508–10
    origin of mankind and, 1457–59,
      1462, 1501, 1504–7
    religious establishments and, 1514
    as republican, 1483, 1495, 1498, 1499
    Sabbath and, 1463–64, 1463*n*, 1470
    scriptures and, 1451–76, 1503, 1504,
      1506
    second administration of, xiii, xvi
    sermons and, 1572
    United States Constitution and,
      1483
    Washington compared to, 1553*n*
    Wortman and, 1525
    Wortman's *Solemn Address to
      Christians and Patriots*, 1479–1528
Jeffersonian Republicans, 884, 1080,
    1478
Jehojada, 16, 756
Jehoram, 756
Jehoshaphat, 33, 217, 955–56
Jehovah. *See* God
Jehu, 716, 724

Jencks, Governor, 359, 367

Jepthae, 753–54, 856, 953, 1403, 1581

Jereboam, 849

Jeremiah, 14, 500, 584, 1422, 1444

Jeroboam, 320, 955, 1423

Jerome of Prague, 204

Jersey, 272, 276, 282, 284

Jersies, 625n

Jerusalem. *See also* Israel
  Amaziah and, 756
  Assyrian king and, 666
  Chaldeans and, 1383
  chosen people and, 586
  destruction of, 40
  divine judgment and, 1439
  fall of, 856
  God's defense of, 217
  Jesus Christ and, 1026
  Jews and, 757
  Nehemiah and, 757
  New Jerusalem, 1055
  repentance of, 567
  Sennacherib's assault on, 534, 666
  tribes of Israel and, 929
  United States compared to, 913–14, 1437
  walls of, 829

Jesuits, 502n, 512, 1370

Jesus Christ. *See also* Gospel;
    Kingdom of Jesus Christ; Laws
    of Jesus Christ
  abuse of, 1536–37
  apocalypse and, 999
  arms of, 201–2
  authority of, 64, 67, 87–88, 90, 117, 1037, 1093
  Belial and, 1474
  chosen people and, 586
  Christian church and, 505
  Christianity's teaching of, 1113
  Christmas and, 1258
  conduct of, 1537–40, 1543
  death and sufferings of, 542, 993, 1036
  defense and defense arms, 727–28, 764–66
  doctrine and, 65
  ecclesiastical government and, 336–37
  ecclesiastical rulers' authority and, 68
  enemies of, 762, 1039, 1090, 1382, 1472
  faith in, 821–22
  first advent of, 1579, 1582, 1585–86
  as foundation for government, 15
  gentiles and, 1034
  Hargrove's *Sermon on the Second Coming of Christ,* 1573–96
  heathens and, 1051
  heroic actions of, 199–200
  historical presence of, 993
  immortality and, 1318–19
  intercession of, 591
  Jerusalem and, 1026
  Jews and, 184–86, 188, 204, 205, 729, 999
  as judge, 186, 206, 356
  justice and, 142
  as king of Jews, 184, 186–90
  laws and, 335–36, 1445
  Lazarus and, 200, 1403
  liberty and, 55, 258
  as Lord of conscience, 65
  love and, 820
  love of, 123
  as mediator, 190–91, 813
  as Messiah, 184, 1579
  ministers and, 63, 68, 76–79, 194, 196, 358, 935
  miracles of, 993
  morality and, 1534

Jesus Christ, *continued*
  Moses and, 957, 963
  nations and, 1052
  non-resistance of, 728
  obedience and, 1071
  officers of, 63
  patriotism and, 1011, 1025–26
  peace and, 1432
  Pilate and, 185
  as pillar, 14, 23
  political oppression of Jews and,
    1431–32
  politics and, 1485
  power of, 86
  preaching of, 821
  purpose of, 995
  redemption of, 584, 1052, 1534
  religious establishment and,
    1098–99
  religious liberty and, 1062
  repentance and, 45, 535–36
  as republican, 1547–48
  resistance and, 727–28
  revolutions and, 1432
  Roman Catholic Church and,
    1354*n*
  rules concerning ministers, 358
  salvation and, 862, 890, 963, 1054
  Samaritan parable of, 1011–12
  Satan and, 199, 994
  second advent of, 999, 1393, 1579,
    1582, 1588–90, 1592, 1595
  sin and, 191–92, 962–63, 1035
  soldiers of, 191, 194–96, 199
  spirit of, 829, 1036–37
  suffering of, 993, 1544
  tax and, 310
  trinity and, 1583
  true religion and, 957
  United States and, 783–84
  war and, 572–73

  William III compared to, 992–95
  as Word, 134
Jethro, 152, 946, 1326, 1328, 1329
Jews. *See also* Israel; Judah; Judaism
  Artaxerxes and, 756–57
  Babylon and, 40, 216, 617, 631–33,
    761, 795, 956–57
  blessings of, 124, 614
  Canaan and, 507, 751, 797, 1050,
    1105, 1392
  as chosen people, 586, 604
  as citizens of Great Britain, 1023
  as civil officers, 1098
  consent of government and,
    634–35
  as converts, 1033–34, 1392
  corruption and, 823
  Cyrus and, 985
  defensive arms use, 744, 751–58
  deliverance from Egypt, 973,
    974–77, 1105, 1117, 1419
  discontent and, 779
  as dissenters, 1092, 1093, 1095
  divine judgments and, 666, 788,
    795, 1335
  divine providence and, 616–17, 758,
    1221, 1419–20
  Edom and, 616
  education of children and,
    955–56, 1223
  Egypt and, 215, 489, 567, 1392, 1419,
    1476
  Egyptian bondage of, 215, 507, 567,
    635, 946, 950, 973
  enemies of, 615–18
  God and, 124, 595, 618–20, 631, 759,
    795, 854, 1189
  Great Britain compared to, 124–25
  Haman and, 665, 758
  honour and, 859
  impiety of, 841–42
  Jerusalem and, 757

Jesus Christ and, 184–86, 188, 204, 205, 729, 999
Jew bill and, 296
Joshua and, 1420
Julian and, 543
Langdon's *Republic of the Israelites an Example to the American States*, 943–67
latter day glory and, 775
laws of, 338
liberty of, 589
Messiah and, 1579
Michael and, 506
ministers of, 342–43
Mosaick Dispensation and, 84
Nebuchadnezzar and, 724
non-conformers to worship and, 346
obedience of, 612–14, 618
patriotism of, 1010–11
Paul and, 1026
persecution of, 743–44
political oppression of, 1431–32
prophecies for, 869
public spirit of, 913
punishment of, 1438
rebellion of, 1476
Red Sea and, 131
restoration of, 620, 893
return to own land, 997, 999–1000
righteousness of, 804
Roman Catholic Church prophecies and, 499
rulers of, 338, 1105–6
Samaritans and, 1011–12, 1036
Samuel and, 125
slavery and, 215, 507, 567, 635, 946, 950, 973, 1050
submission and, 540
theocracy of, 1037
in United States, 1392
Washington and, 1182*n*

wilderness and, 1392, 1420
wrath of men and, 663
Zion and, 1567
Joab, 360, 553, 1399
Joash, 756, 954
Job, 706, 887
Joel, 755, 1588, 1589
John, Saint
fasting and, 34
Jesus Christ and, 1583
as pillar, 14
prophecies of, 497–98, 504–5, 510, 655–56, 1444
Roman Catholic Church and, 499
John (king of England), 320, 447, 476, 750
John I (king of Portugal), 1038
John II (king of Portugal), 1040
Johnson, 1551
Johnson, Samuel
British colonies and, 425
government and, 429
Jefferson and, 1510*n*
laws and, 427
voting and, 430
Wesley and, 410, 422, 424, 426, 432
John the Baptist, 576
John the Cicero, 1089–90
Jonah, 29–30, 32
Jonathan, 754, 1402–3, 1414*n*
Joseph
Egypt and, 663, 777, 973
good out of evil and, 260
house of, 1423
lusts of men and, 663
noble actions and, 893
presence of God and, 219
Reuben and, 590, 592
Washington as, xxiv

Joshua
  Amalek and, 572
  assurances of, 932
  church-state relations and, 1487
  Connecticut governor as, 858
  covenant and, 634–36
  Gibeonites and, 1050
  Israel's government and, 952, 954,
    1326
  Jews and, 1420
  as pillar, 16
  sun arrested in course, 780
  Washington as, 784, 786
Judah. *See also* Israel; Jews; Judaism
  defensive arms as duty and, 762
  divine judgments and, 1439
  divine providence and, 594
  envy and, 875
  fighting in cause of virtue, 571
  forsaking God and, 230
  God's cause and, 589
  Greece and, 761
  Israel's restoration and, 784
  Jeroboam and, 955
  Philistines and, 754
  power abuse and, 567
  sins of tyrants and, 743
  United States compared to, 1437
Judaism. *See also* Jews
  advent and, 1594–95
  Christian church distinguished
    from, 1033, 1579–80
  church-state relations and,
    945–46, 950, 955, 957
  corruption of, 954, 956, 1034
  divine revelation and, 1578
  Dunbar and, 208
  French Revolution and, 1350
  God and, 962, 1419
  idolatry and, 946, 949, 954, 955,
    1062

Jesus Christ's kingdom and, 205
  mourning and, 1402–3
Judas, 360
Judas Iscariot, 1480, 1482
Judas Maccabeus, 745
Jude, Saint, 1583
Judea, 633, 993
Judges. *See also* Courts
  appointment of, 324
  British ministry and, 319
  corruption in, 960, 1520
  as era of Israel, 952–55
  impartiality of, 389
  Israel's government and, 947, 1326,
    1420
  Jesus Christ as judge, 186, 206
  power of, 318–22
  presence of God and, 226–28
Judgments. *See also* Divine judg-
    ments; Right of private
    judgment
  differences in, 1089, 1090
  fasting and, 33–36
  presence of God and, 227
  reading with, 901–2, 904
  religious establishment and, 1088
  in religious matters, 61–67
  resistance and, 726
  scientific research and, 898
  against tyranny in scriptures,
    598–99
  unity of, in Christianity, 825
  of Washington, 1412
Judicial branch. *See* Courts
Judicial infatuation, 668–69, 671
Julian (emperor of Rome), 203, 338,
    543
Junius, 1520*n*
Jupiter as pagan god, 1195, 1257
Jure divino. See Divine right

Jus Populi, 731, 755, 758

Jus Populi Vindicatum, 720

Justice
in adversity, 840
Chauncy's *Civil Magistrates Must Be Just, Ruling in the Fear of God*, 139–77
conscience and, 1063, 1429
defense of state and, 162–63, 172
defensive arms as duty and, 760
elections and, 1065
enjoyment of United States as good land and, 875–76
eternal rules of, 386–87, 396–98
executive branch of government and, 861
foreign war and, 162–63
of God's sovereign rule over nations, 804
heathens and, 1201–2
impartial distribution of, 383
injustice, 845–49, 860
Isaiah and, 837
laws and, 147–54, 918, 1331, 1429
for liberties and priviledges, 156–62, 172
ministers and, 159–62
national debt and, 154–56, 389
natural, 145, 1115
patriotism and, 1012
political slavery and, 1158
power and, 146–47
in prosperity, 840
public administration and, 1066
religious tyranny and, 1063–64
of rulers, 145–66, 385–92
slavery and, 1158
Stamp Act repeal and, 251
trade and, 150–51, 173–74
true religion and, 1253
war and, 572

welfare and, 163–64
Juvenal, 1159

Kames, Lord. *See* Home, Henry
Kamschatka, 1505
Kamskatka, 1178
Kant, Immanuel, 1006
Keilah, 755
Kent, James, 1478
Kentucky, 328, 1046n
Keteltas, Abraham
biographical information on, 580
God Arising and Pleading His People's Cause, 581–605
Thursday Lecture and, xxiii
Kingdom of Jesus Christ
church-state relations and, 341, 357, 1485
compared to earthly kingdoms, 193–94, 199, 201–5, 729, 861
Davies's *Mediatorial Kingdom and Glories of Jesus Christ*, 181–206
glories of, 620
in hearts of men, 822
promotion of, 830
Kingdoms
of antichrist, 893
arms of, 201–2
colonial ancestors and, 445
disputes of, 183
founded in blood, 197
God's power over, 614
God's sovereignty over, 796–804
interference in, 1053
against Jesus Christ, 192
kingdom of God, 586
kingdom of heaven, 190
kings alienating, 731
religious establishment and, 1087, 1088

Kingdoms, *continued*
  rights of, 654–55
  of Satan, 191, 501
  universal, 193
  whore of Babylon and, 515
  of the world, 525
King of Great Britain. *See* British
    Crown; and names of specific
    kings
Kings. *See also* British Crown;
    Monarchy; Rulers; and names
    of specific kings
  alienating kingdoms, 731
  allegiance to, 451–54
  assassination of, 1204
  authority of, 315, 323, 767
  of Canaan, 759, 768
  colonial Americans and, 451–56,
    460
  divine right doctrine and, 383, 632,
    1021, 1176, 1181
  dominion of, 1027
  as era of Israel, 955–56
  fiduciary power of, 737
  French Revolution and, 1180
  God and, 316, 664, 767
  God as Israel's king, 948, 955
  God as sovereign of world, 611–12,
    786–87, 794, 795, 796–804, 810–12
  honoring of, 251–52, 1019
  Isaiah's prophecies and, 1420
  Israel's demand for, 636, 1326, 1420,
    1547
  Jesus Christ's kingdom and, 729
  laws and, 731–32, 918, 950
  ministers and, 342–43
  as nursing fathers of the Church,
    125, 346
  ordinance of majestracy and,
    721–22, 767
  pardon of criminals, 986
  people's conditions unto, 736–37

  power and, 321, 737–38
  prayer against, 767
  protection of subjects and, 452
  rebellion of, 1017
  religion and, 357*n*
  resistance to, 720–21
  rights and, 383
  role of, 316–17, 323–24, 488
  Roman Catholic Church and, 499
  Satan and, 500
  as servants, 1017
  statues of, 1261
  supplication to, 729–30
  taxation and, 419, 431–32
  tyranny of, 730, 731, 732
  war and, 574–76, 724–25
  will as law, 950
  wrongdoings of, 706
King's College, 816
Kingston, 625*n*
Kirkham, Donald H., 412
Knigge, 1389
Knowledge. *See also* Wisdom
  chain of, 890
  Christian knowledge, 1115, 1125
  church-state relations, 1122
  dignity of man and, 890–91, 1071
  of divine perfections, 949
  education and, 878, 880, 961
  freedom of the press and, 987
  of gospel, 1091, 1438, 1580
  government and, 1410
  immutable boundaries of, 895–97
  independence and, 638
  of laws, 1328
  liberty and, 900, 1071–73
  libraries and, 900–901
  man's capacity for, 890–91
  military forces and, 1138–39, 1140
  patriotism and, 1013–14

philosophers and, 1133
of religion, 1318
religion compared to, 898
of right and wrong, 1192–93
rulers and, 1331
of salvation, 987
Solomon and, 891, 906
subjects of human inquiry, 896–97
true religion and, 1181
Knox, Mr., 756, 763
Korah, 722, 780
Kuklick, Bruce, 884

Laban, 590
Labrador, 1505
Lacedemonians, 1204–5
Lachish, 756
La Fayette, Marquis de, 1262, 1281, 1297
Laish, 1134–35, 1139, 1141, 1143, 1383, 1431
Lamb, blood of, 506, 521
Lamech, 19
Lancaster, England, 1043
Lancaster, house of, 1297, 1510
Land. *See also* Property
French Revolution and, 1248–49
land rights, 728, 741
Lathrop's *Sermon on a Day
Appointed for Publick
Thanksgiving*, 867–81
taxation of, 282, 324
title to, 457
United States as good land, 869–73
Landgrave of Hesse, 748
Langdon, Samuel
biographical information on, 942
*Republic of the Israelites an Example
to the American States*, 943–67
Lathrop, 1355n

Lathrop, Joseph
biographical information on, 866
*Sermon on a Day Appointed for
Publick Thanksgiving*, 867–81
Latter day glory, 775, 1098. *See also*
Second advent
Laud, William, 1486n
Laurens, Henry, 785
Law, John, 1248
Law of liberty, xvi, xvin. *See also*
Liberty
Law of Moses
authority of, 340n
cases of inconsiderable value and, 951
church-state relations and, 345
colonists' use of, 338
government by law and, 950
Israel's consent to, 634
Israel's observance of, 945–46
Israel's practice of, 957
Israel's worship and, 335
Jesus Christ's superseding of, 184
Rehoboam and, 955
Laws. *See also* Law of Moses; Laws
of God; Laws of Jesus Christ;
Laws of nature; Obedience to
laws
agrarian, 1175
as aid for defense of truth, 1090
atheism and, 1462
authority and, 467–69
British constitution and, 295
British legislation and, 465
British Parliament and, 274, 279,
282, 322, 379n, 400, 487, 492, 599,
799
of Caligula, 1090
ceremonial, 1062
certificate law, 1093–94, 1097, 1098
changeable nature of, 918

Laws, *continued*
changes and, 918
against Christianity, 388
church established by, 992
civil injuries and, 1516
civil officers and, 1070, 1329–30
civil society/civil union and,
65–66, 383, 386, 917, 923
coercive, xx
for colonial America, 425–26
colonial assemblies and, 464
consent and, 413–14, 427
constitutions and, 387, 1084–85
for the disobedient, 1084
divine compared with human, 194
dominion of, 1027
duty to God and, 1093
ecclesiastical laws and, 274, 276
enactment of, 386–89
eternal, xxiv
every law not contrary to superior
law, 81–83
execution of, 151–54, 386, 389–90
feudal system and, 950
foreign, 1176
free power of, 415
French Revolution and, 1265, 1297,
1298, 1347
fundamental laws, 918
gospel and, 1094–95
government and, 387
of Great Britain, 276, 308, 309,
950–51
happiness and, 1065–66
imperfection of, 1156
of Israel, 946
Jacobin Society and, 1242
Jesus Christ and, 335–36, 1445
justice and, 147–54, 918, 1331, 1429
of kingdoms of world, 193–94
kings and, 731–32, 918, 950
knowledge of, 1328

laws of Jesus Christ distinguished
from, 1095
legally proved actions and, 1108
liberty and, 728, 1077
limitation on kings' power and,
737–38
ministers and, 340–43
ministers' salaries and, 1091, 1094,
1095–96, 1097–98
morality and, 1116, 1268
moral law, 133–34, 948, 996
Muhammad and, 1093
of nations, 1271
noninterference of, 990–91
oppression and, 1427
penal, 388, 389, 488, 1022
of plantations, 466
principles of, 1563
property and, 1249, 1517
protection of, 812
provincial, 415–16
public faith and, 650
purpose of, 1016
reason and, 1331
reform of, 1442
religious establishment and, 1083,
1092–93
religious liberty and, 339–40,
347–49, 356
representation and, 1065, 1066, 1084
resistance to oppression and,
724–25, 734–35
revenue and, 1178
rights and, 446–47
Rome and Roman Empire, 469,
950, 1175, 1281
rulers and, 386, 393, 1084, 1330
of Scotland, 272, 274, 275
of society, 59, 383
sovereignty of the people and,
959, 1064–65, 1175
taxation and, 287, 426

trade and commerce and, 149
tyranny and, 148, 722, 735
United States government and,
    957
Laws of God
    arbitrary government and, 59
    Bible and, 1476
    Christianity and, 1192
    civil society/civil union and,
        914–18
    conduct and, 1466
    consistency of, 735
    defensive arms and, 768
    disobedience of, 948
    duties to man and, 743
    happiness and, 914
    laws of Creator, xx, 391
    laws of Jehovah, 917–18
    liberty of conscience and, 1467
    obedience to, 564, 614, 1424
    public virtue and, 805
    punishments and, 611
    religion and, 339
    resistance to oppression and,
        724–25, 923
    rights and, 383
    rulers and, 391
    taxation and, 311
    tyranny and, 305
    virtue and, 1318, 1320
Laws of Jesus Christ
    church officers and, 78–79
    church-state relations and, 81
    Jesus Christ's authority and, 88
    justice and, 164–65
    laws of state and, 84, 86, 1095
    love as, 996
    moral law and, 133–34, 996
    righteousness and, 743
    Roman Catholic Church and, 1096
    scriptures and, 193–94

social conduct and, 875
    worship and, 69–71
Laws of nature
    application of, 57–59
    civil society/civil union and, 917
    colonial America and, 310, 323, 741
    defense and, 263, 726, 734–35, 768
    domination and, 536
    flood and, 1502, 1504
    laws of God and, 915
    plea in court and, 733
    religion and, 894
    resistance to oppression and,
        724–25
    subjects' rights and, 383
    tyranny and, 735
Lazarus, 200, 1335, 1403
Learning. See Education; Knowledge
Le Brun, 1269, 1286
Lee, General, 574
Leeds, Duke of, 276, 1521
Legislation. See Laws
Legislature and legislators. See also
        British Parliament; Continental
        Congress; United States
        Congress
    altering constitutions and, 1085
    colonial, 415
    of Connecticut, 859
    corruption in, 960
    education and, 933, 1121–22
    fear of God and, 960
    individual oppression and, 1442
    justice and, 387–89
    legislative branch's balanced pow-
        ers, 802, 1176, 1343
    liberty of conscience and, 1097
    ministers' salaries and, 366
    in monarchy, 1177
    morality and, 1120–21

Legislature and legislators, *continued*
  nonconformists and, 1094
  reformation of laws and, 1330–31
  religious establishment and,
    1093–94
  righteousness of, 933
  of states, 1232, 1277
  taxation without representation
    and, 356
Le Grand, René, 1389
Leland, John
  Backus and, 328, 1080
  biographical information on, 1080,
    1082
  Rights of Conscience Inalienable,
    1081–99
Lepidus, 1204
Lesna, Poland, 749
Levites, 595, 618, 913, 953, 1429
Levy, Leonard, 1478
Lewis the Little, 1406
Lexington, Battle of, xxiv, 692,
    779, 799
Lexington, Massachusetts
  Cumings's *Sermon Preached at
    Lexington on the 19th of April*,
    659–81
  Cushing's *Divine Judgments upon
    Tyrants*, 609–26
Lex Rex, 720, 755
Libertinism, 1124
Liberty. *See also* Civil liberties;
    Freedom; Liberty of
    conscience; Religious liberty;
    Rights
  abolitionism and, 1053, 1054
  acting to one's own will, 56
  Adams and, 1499–1500, 1526
  Allen's *Oration upon the Beauties of
    Liberty*, 303–25

American Revolution and, 778,
    1053, 1313, 1314
  anarchy and, 1016, 1180
  arbitrary government and, 443
  British colonies and, 270
  British constitution and, 273, 286,
    290–91, 297–98, 427, 476, 871
  British Crown's desire for absolute
    monarchy and, 777
  cap of, 1256
  cause of God and, 596
  charters and charter rights and,
    305, 402
  Christianity and, 597–99, 1036,
    1154–60, 1163, 1167
  church-state relations and, 1126
  civil society/civil union and, 388
  cockade of, 1260–61
  of colonial America, 240, 241, 292,
    378, 419–20, 440, 481, 970
  colonial America's cause and, 603,
    731
  colonial ancestors and, 1312, 1546,
    1567
  comparisons of, 1497
  constitutions and, 1299
  costs of, 639–40
  defensive arms and, 725, 728, 1135
  despotism and, 1072
  education and, 649
  enemies of, 1072
  enthusiasm and, 1243, 1245, 1254,
    1260, 1261
  equality and, 1064
  Europe and, 1027, 1054, 1163
  Evans's *Sermon Delivered at the
    Annual Election*, 1059–78
  evils and, 1126
  factions and, 1267, 1278, 1294
  feelings of, 1559–60, 1568
  France and, 482, 997, 1027, 1071,
    1076, 1299

free government based on, xxiv,
263–64, 382, 596
French literary men and, 1252
French Revolution and, 1163–64,
1179–80, 1268–70, 1357
Glorious Revolution and, 476,
970, 985–88
as God-given, xx, 325
gospel and, 1062
government and, xxiv, 58–59,
263–64, 331–35, 382, 596, 1037,
1142, 1155
gratitude for, 1074
Great Britain and, 320, 402,
596–97, 602–3, 639, 970, 1027, 1313
Greece and, 1016, 1160n
grounds for war and, 726
happiness and, 1061
history and, 1016, 1075–76
independence and, 1061
internal, 681
Jesus Christ and, 55, 258
of Jews, 589
justice and, 156–62
knowledge and, 900, 1071–73
law of, xvi, xvin
laws and, 728, 1077
licentiousness and, 486, 1074, 1125,
1320, 1566
limitations on, 1421–22
love of, 1312–13, 1421
luxury and, 1026
man's destruction and, 1429
military forces in defense of, 1135
national virtue and, 878
as natural right, 445
obedience and, 1071
obedience to laws and, 1319
oppression and, xix, 305, 306
pagans and, 1160
pamphlets written in support of,
591

parting with, to preserve rest, 1084
party spirit and, 1274–75
patriotism and, 1013, 1015–16, 1025,
1026, 1075
peace and, 651
personal liberty, 918
perversion of, 824
piety and, 1111
planted in colonial America, 524
political, 878
preserving of, by altering government, 1085
pretender and, 396
price of, 937
principles of, 602–3, 1036
protection of, 1068–78
Puritans and, 1161n
rational, 915–16
reason and, 486
religion as preserver of, 1073–74
religious truth and, xiv, 61–67, 81
representation and, 1024
Rhode Island and, 307
right of private judgment and, 55,
61–67
Rome and, 1160n
rulers opposing, 760
societies' infringement on, 1233
sovereignty of the people and,
644–45, 1153
Spanish Armada and, 983
spirit of, 384
spiritual liberty, 1154–55
spread of, 1053
of subjects, 1421
submission of colonial America
and, 720
taxation and representation,
1067–68
threats to, 399
trade and commerce and, 490, 516
treason and, 1297

Liberty, *continued*
  true liberty of man, 331–32
  truth and, xx, xxiv
  tyranny and, 334, 392, 691, 986,
    1071–72, 1313
  United States and, 833, 1071, 1076
  United States Constitution and,
    871, 957, 972, 1061, 1343–44
  United States government and,
    643
  vice and, 992
  virtue and, 1074
  Voltaire and, 1252
  war and, 483
  Williams's *Essential Rights and
    Liberties of Protestants*, 53–118
  of worship, 404
  worth of, 1061
  wrath of Great Britain and, 673
  youth and, 1074
Liberty of conscience. *See also*
    Conscience
  advantages of, 404
  alienable versus inalienable,
    1085–86
  Backus and, 328
  British ministry and, 403
  charters and charter rights and,
    344, 364
  Christianity and, 1035
  church-state relations and, 339,
    990
  Glorious Revolution and, 987–88,
    1021
  government and, 1518
  Jefferson and, 1516
  laws of God and, 1467
  legislators and, 1097
  Leland's *Rights of Conscience
    Inalienable*, 1081–99
  magistrates and, 1517
  ministers' salaries and, 1095, 1097

  religion and, 1121
  religious liberty and, 362, 364–66
  southern states and, 1099
  suffrage and, 1465–68
  United States Constitution and,
    1518
  United States government and,
    1182
Libnah, 756
Licentiousness
  civil liberty and, 1179
  civil officers and, 1213
  in France, 1298
  freedom and, 1036, 1440
  French Revolution and, 1264, 1265
  infidelity and, 1464
  liberty and, 486, 1074, 1125, 1566
  republican government and, 1319,
    1320
  ridicule of religion and, 1108
  of rulers, 1424
Licinius, 750
Linn, William, 1448, 1480, 1481–82,
    1493
Liston, 1526, 1528
Littleton, 1493
Liverpool, England, 1043
Livingston, William, 702
Loanda, 1042
Loango, 1041
Locke, John
  accomplishments of, 899
  on civil liberty, 258, 639
  knowledge and, 1014
  natural rights and, 330
  noble actions and, 893
  as philosopher, 1312
  Williams and, 54, 61
Lombards, 750
London, England

Constitutional Answer to Wesley's Calm Address, 423–38

Fletcher's *Bible and the Sword*, 561–78

Price's *Discourse on the Love of Our Country*, 1005–28

slave trade and, 1043

Winchester's *Century on the Glorious Revolution*, 971–1000

Long Island, 787

Longo, 1041*n*

Lopos, Cape, 1041

Lords. *See* British House of Lords

Lord's people. *See* Chosen people of God

Lot, 590, 593, 751

Louis, Saint, 1346

Louis IX (king of France), 750

Louis XIV (king of France), 1240

Louis XVI (king of France)
accomplishments of, 651
French Revolution and, 1181
murder of, 1390
United States alliance and, 699, 746–47, 785–86, 801

Louis XVII (king of France), 1294

Louisbourg, 52, 122, 134, 214, 478

Louisiana, 478

Louisiana Purchase, xvi

Love
Christianity and, 1011, 1025
duty to, 1093
of enemies, 1011
faith and, 827
fruit of, 827
of God to men, 1316–17
hearts of men and, 827–28
of importance, 1088
of Jesus Christ, 123
law of, 331, 832, 915
liberty and, 992, 1312–13
religion and, 1111
sins and, 934–35
spirit of, 820
true religion and, 895

Love of country. *See* Patriotism

Loyalty
to British Crown, 296, 313, 325, 381, 397*n*, 399, 474–75, 671, 720
spirit of, 384

Lusts of men, 661–66, 680

Luther, Martin, 83, 204, 893

Lutherans, 1263

Luxury
civilization and, 1196
corruption of, 1077, 1390
industry and, 876
irreligion and, 1337
liberty and, 1026
prosperity and, 852–53
religious support and, 831
taxation and, 1068

Lycurgus, 133, 950

Lyons, 1265, 1346, 1384–85

Lysias, 158

Maccabees, 744, 761, 1380

Macedonians, 813, 850

Macedonius, 746

Macpherson, 785

Madison, Bishop James
biographical information on, 1306
Manifestations of the Beneficence of Divine Providence Towards America, 1307–20

Madison, James
  Backus and, 328
  days of prayer, fasting, and
    thanksgiving proclamations,
    xxiv
  Evans and, 1058
  Federal Convention and, xxiv
  government and, xx
  Leland and, 1080
  Bishop James Madison and, 1306
  Witherspoon and, 532
  Wortman and, 1478
Magdeburgh, 748
Magistrates. *See also* Civil officers
  advancement of religion and, 1116,
    1211–13
  authority of, 724–25
  Chauncy's *Civil Magistrates Must
    Be Just, Ruling in the Fear of God*,
    139–77
  choice of, 1066, 1177
  citizens' complaints and, 930–31
  conscience and, 925, 931
  contempt of, 1016–19
  duty and, 724, 922, 1089
  effects on community, 1107
  factions and, 936
  in free government, 925
  French Revolution and, 1351
  fundamental laws and, 918
  God's guidance and, 926, 930
  justice of, 141
  lawfulness of, 741
  liberty of conscience and, 1517
  ministers' relationship with,
    933–35, 1117, 1118
  motives of, 926
  obedience of, 1016–17, 1108, 1430,
    1432, 1496
  oppression and, 724
  peace and, 934

  personal example of, 1115–16, 1119–21,
    1211
  as pillars of earth, 21–22
  power of, 737
  prayer for, 935
  private retaliation and, 727
  purpose of, 1016
  rebellion against, 722
  respect for, 1016
  restraining vice, 1142
  righteousness and, 931
  as servants of people, 1017
  subjection to, 722–24
  submission to, 1019
  as tyrants, 722
  vice and, 1189–90
  virtue and, 1189
  Weare and, 802
Magna Charta
  British Parliament and, 599
  colonial America and, 240, 426
  colonial constitutions and, 471
  liberty and, 320–21
  reading of, 447
  right of private judgment and, 117
  trial by jury and, 428
Magnalia, B., 363*n*
Magog, 860
Mahomedans. *See* Muhammadanism
Mahomet. *See* Muhammad
Maine, 1045*n*
Malindo, 1041*n*
Man, Island of, 272, 276
Manasseh, 635, 636, 743
Manheim, 1376
*Manifestations of the Beneficence of
  Divine Providence Towards
  America* (Madison), 1307–20

Mankind. *See also* Dignity of man; Hearts of men; Passions of men; Wrath of men
  accountability to God, 1191, 1192
  angels and, 889–90
  blessings of human nature, 1012–16
  brotherhood of, 1113
  care of himself and, 1377–79
  charity and, 1429
  constancy of human nature, 850–51
  contradiction and, 1451–52
  death and, 1400
  depravity of, 915, 1429
  destruction and, 1429
  duty of, 832, 1360
  fallen, 1430
  fallibility of, 77–78, 382
  fear of God and, 1430
  God and, 1077, 1316–17
  harmony of, 820
  Jesus Christ as mediator for, 190–91, 1325
  lusts of, 661–66, 680
  as microcosm, 1593
  mind of, 1254
  mortality of, 1401
  order and, 145
  origin of, 1457–59, 1462, 1504–7
  as pillars, 16
  rights of, 922
  ruling over own spirit, 1431
  worship and, 69
Manks laws, 276
Manly, 1391
Manners
  children's education and, 1442
  depravity of, 1213
  factions and, 1231
  French Revolution and, 1247, 1265
  independence and, 1561–62, 1568

  religion and, 1566
  simplicity of, 1159
Mansfield, 691, 695, 704, 705
Manslaughter, 948
Mantinians, 746
Manufactures, 241, 1228, 1249–50, 1347, 1564
Manumission. *See* Slavery of Negroes
Manumission Society, 1478
Manwaring, 248
Mara, 1494
Marah, 982
Marat, Jean Paul, 1261, 1281, 1297, 1383, 1497
Marcota, 746
Marius, 1203, 1279, 1281–83, 1297
Marriage, 918, 1113–14, 1264, 1376
Marseilles, 1265, 1296
Marshall, John, 1340
Martin V, 1038, 1039
Martinico, 1043*n*
Martyrol, 749
Martyrs. *See also* Persecutions
  of American freedom, 785
  of Christian church, 842, 1198
  Protestants and Protestantism and, 198–99
  resistance and, 728
  Roman Catholic Church and, 1257
  self-defense and, 745
  Stephen as, 1403
Mary, Queen of Scots, 134
Mary I (queen of England), 117, 503, 988
Maryland, 1046*n*. *See also* Baltimore, Maryland
Mason, John, 1448

Mason, John Mitchell
  biographical information on, 1448
  Griswold and, 1530
  Linn and, 1448, 1480
  Voice of Warning to Christians, 1449–76
Masons, 1275, 1278–79, 1373–74, 1413
Massachusetts. *See also* Boston, Massachusetts
  Backus's *Appeal to the Public for Religious Liberty*, 329–68
  Backus's banishment from, 345
  Chauncy's *Civil Magistrates Must Be Just, Ruling in the Fear of God*, 139–77
  church-state relations and, 1118, 1122
  constitution of, 629–56, 1118, 1130
  Dunbar's *The Presence of God with His People*, 209–30
  election sermons preached in, xxii
  Emmons's *Dignity of Man*, 885–907
  Great Britain's tyranny and, 725
  Keteltas's *God Arising and Pleading His People's Cause*, 581–605
  Lathrop's *Sermon on a Day Appointed for Publick Thanksgiving*, 867–81
  legislature of, 340
  military forces of, 1135
  pedobaptism and, 344, 347, 367
  population breakdown of, 1045n
  rebellion and, 697
  religious establishment in, 1086
  religious liberty in, 1080
  Roman Catholic Church and, 1359n
  tyranny and, 480
Massachusetts-Bay colony, 416, 420, 432–33
Massachusetts Historical Society, 1130

Massaniello of Naples, 420, 438
Mather, Cotton, 8, 26, 208, 341n, 343
Mather, Increase, 8
Mather, Moses
  America's Appeal to the Impartial World, 441–92
  biographical information on, 440
Matignon, Rev., 1349n
Matthias, 744–45, 749
Maximus, 746
Mayhew, Jonathan
  biographical information on, 232
  Snare Broken, 233–64
Mazzei, 1462–63, 1483, 1501, 1510–14, 1513n
McClintock, Samuel
  biographical information on, 790
  Sermon on Occasion of the Commencement of the New-Hampshire Constitution, xxii, 791–813
McLoughlin, William G., 328
Mede, 898
Medes, 758, 813, 1329
The Mediatorial Kingdom and Glories of Jesus Christ (Davies), 181–206
Mediterranean, 272, 284
Melinda, 1041
Mendon, 357, 360
Mentz, 1375
Mercies of Heaven. *See* Divine providence
Merimac River, 477
Meroz, curse of, 721, 759, 785, 1138
Meshac, 590
Messiah, 184, 186, 188, 1579. *See also* Jesus Christ
Metaphysics, 897, 1107

Methodism, xvii, 412, 560

Mexico, 594, 982, 1160*n*, 1313

Mezeray, Monsieur, 482

Micah, 315–16, 954

Michael, 506, 523*n*, 574

Midian and Midianites, 594, 752, 763, 954, 973, 1326

Military forces. *See also* British army and navy; Colonial militia; Defense and Defensive arms; Resistance; War
  of American Revolution, xvi
  defense of liberty and, 1135, 1145
  discipline of, 1146
  duty and, 555–56
  of French Revolution, 1244, 1245, 1267
  God and, 213, 214, 227, 1147
  of Israel, 946, 953–54
  John the Baptist and, 576
  knowledge and, 1138–39
  military institutions, 1561, 1568
  military officers, 1213
  military offices, 1022
  as needful burden on public, 575–76
  oppression and, 872
  payment of, 847–48
  public expenses and, 1521
  remembrance of, 785, 1568
  resistance to, 741–42
  ships of war, 548, 548–49*n*
  of Spain, 983

Militia. *See* Colonial militia

Millenium, 1000, 1353*n*

Miller, John, 1150

Miller, Perry, xvii

Miller, Samuel
  biographical information on, 1150

Sermon on the Anniversary of the Independence of America, 1151–67

Milo, 1202

Milton, John, 51, 258, 898, 1014, 1310*n*, 1566*n*

Minden, 694, 698, 706, 799

Ministers. *See also* Ministers' salaries
  American Revolution, role of, xiii, 779, 862, 1315
  character of, 1485–86, 1488
  choice of, 100–102, 873, 964, 966, 1092
  as citizens, 1494
  civil rulers and, 1116–17, 1336–37
  of Connecticut, 861–62
  duty of, 1123–25, 1443–44, 1485
  examination of, 111, 114
  example of, 1215
  Hamilton and, 1499*n*
  influence of, 1481
  instruction and, 1214–15
  Jesus Christ and, 63, 68, 76–79, 194, 196, 358, 935
  justice and, 159–62
  as king's ministers, 342–43
  law and, 340–43, 340*n*
  magistrates' relationship with, 933–35, 1117, 1118
  in Massachusetts, 340
  New Light or Side, xix
  Old Light or Side, xix
  as pillars of church, 14
  plantations and, 341
  political parties and, 1481, 1489, 1494
  political prosperity and, 1214–15
  politics and, 1466, 1485–86, 1492–94
  power over church, 105–6
  preaching out of parish, 52, 103, 107, 112–14
  presence of God and, 228–30

Ministers, *continued*
  punishment of, 106–11
  religious promotion of, 934
  right to assistance, 104–5, 108
  role of, xiv, 317
  salvation and, 934
  scriptures and, 1506
  as soldiers, 191, 196
  suffrages of, 1486
  union among, 935
  United States Constitution and,
    1525*n*
  virtue and, 935
  warrants for, 354
Ministers' salaries
  charters and, 1093
  choice of ministers and, 366–68,
    989
  in Connecticut, 1092
  Constantine the Great and, 1088
  contracts for, 1094, 1095–96, 1441
  dissenters and, 1095
  Great Britain and, 1083
  Jefferson and, 1464
  laws and, 1091, 1097–98
  legislature and, 366
  liberty of conscience and, 1095, 1097
  religious establishment and, 1091
  religious liberty and, 356, 360–62,
    366, 989
  Rhode Island and, 1094–95, 1094*n*,
    1097
  rulers' care and, 159–62
  subject to king and, 341
  support for, 849, 964, 989
  taxation and, 342–43, 342*n*,
    346–48, 352, 355, 366*n*, 368, 1097
Minorca, 272, 284
Miracles, 982, 993, 1503, 1503*n*, 1504
Missingomo, 1041*n*
Mithridates, 1281, 1282, 1283

Moab, 33
Mode of trial. *See* Trial by jury
Mohammedism. *See*
  Muhammadanism
Mohican Indians, 1186
Molesworth, Lord, 276
Moliere, 298
Moloch, 1500
Monarchy. *See also* Aristocracy;
    British Crown; Kings
  absolute, 1054
  balance of power and, 1177
  Christianity and, 1086
  divine rights of kings doctrine,
    383, 632, 1021, 1176, 1181
  education and, 1181
  Fenno and, 1527
  as form of government, 1327
  France's calendar and, 1258
  free government and, 1272
  French republican party and, 1295
  French Revolution and, 1180, 1181,
    1253, 1262, 1269, 1271, 1497
  Hamilton and, 1524, 1527
  hereditary, 1083, 1269, 1435, 1437
  Jacobin Society and, 1262, 1287
  Jews and, 1037
  men of ambition and, 1230
  oppression and, 1562
  republican government versus,
    1359
  scriptures and, 1547
Money
  love of, 400, 769–70, 992
  paper, 174, 938–39, 966
  Spain and, 982–83
Monmouth, battle of, 781
Monongahela, 1407
Montague, 368

Montesquieu, Charles, 295, 1014,
1161n, 1176
Montgomery, 653, 785
Moore, Dr., 1178
Morality. See also Virtue
Christianity and, 1113, 1166, 1183, 1189,
1191, 1196
corruption of, 841, 842
deists and, 1332
enemies and, 1538–40
Epictetus and, 1200n
factions and, 1231
free government and, 1410
French Revolution and, 1239,
1264–66
of God, 981, 1193–94, 1207, 1209, 1211
happiness and, 1105
Illuminati and, 1374
Jesus Christ and, 1534
laws and, 1116, 1268
laws of God and, 914, 916
of legislators, 1120–21
of magistrates, 1107
man blessed with moral sense, xx
Masons and, 1373
moral perfections of God, 888,
1193–94, 1207, 1208, 1209, 1211
of nations, 795, 796, 804–6
of New England, 1561
pagan gods and, 1195
patriotism and, 1024–25
of people, 1213
philosophical, 1108, 1318
political, 1317
political prosperity and, 1189, 1191,
1410
public administration and, 917, 1121,
1378
public injustice and, 849
reason and, 1410
religion and, 966, 1268, 1410

righteousness of nations and, 965
of Roman Catholic Church, 1354n
of Rome, 804–5
of rulers, 1424
scriptures and, 1105
ten commandments and, 946
war's effects on, 1265
Washington and, 1405, 1408
Mordecai, 217, 590, 665, 758
Mordecai the Jew, 541
Morse, Dr., 1355n
Mortality, 880, 1401
Moses. See also Law of Moses
Aaron and, 1105, 1127, 1326, 1443
aristocracy and, 920–21
authority of, 1506
burden of government and, 946
burning bush and, 631
choice of rulers and, 1329
church-state relations and, 1118, 1127
conduct of, 977
Connecticut governor as, 858
defensive arms as duty and, 760
dignity of man and, 895
divine judgment and, 1335
flood and, 1502
God's aid in military enterprises
and, 595
God's mercy and judgment, 612
God's name and, 978
God's pleading cause through, 590
God's spirit and, 779
government appointments and, 152
impiety and, 841
inspiration of, 1117
Israel's constitution and, 645, 945
Israel's deliverance from Egypt
and, 976–77
Israel's senate and, 952
Jesus Christ and, 957, 963
Jews under, 1033

Moses, *continued*
  Korah and, 722
  Mosaic history, 1457
  Mosaic principles, 1051, 1052
  Mosaic ritual, 1033
  Mosaick Dispensation, 84
  noble actions and, 893
  ordinances of, 1033
  persecution and, 521
  Pharaoh's daughter and, 592, 973
  as pillar, 14, 16, 17
  prayer and, 36, 572
  presence of God and, 229
  ritual of, 1034
  as ruler, 1106, 1325–26, 1330, 1336
  scriptures and, 1454
  tribal government and, 947
  veil and, 1593, 1594
  wilderness and, 1420
  wisdom and, 837
Mosheim, 1487
Mount Enon Academy, 1396
Mount Ephraim, 752
Mount Nitria, 746
Mount of Olives, 999
Mount Vernon, 1413, 1414
Mozambique coast, 1041
Mugford, 1391
Muhammad, 1083, 1093
Muhammadanism
  Christian enslavement and, 1263
  Jesus Christ's kingdom and, 205
  National Convention of France
    compared to, 1262
  in Persia, 1392
  rise of, 990, 1538
  subduing of, 893
  United States and, 1191
Munster, 361

Naboth, 320, 323, 598
Nantes, 1384–85
Nantz, 1347
Naphtali, Surveyor of, 720, 731–33, 759
Naples, 1371
Natablus, 756
Nathan, 1499*n*
National debt
  colonial America and, 240, 777
  common debts, 346
  fairness and, 1115
  French Revolution and, 1247–48
  of Great Britain, 649, 777, 809,
    847, 847*n*, 1026, 1521
  injustice and, 845–46
  justice and, 154–56, 389
  paper money and, 938–39, 966
  payment of, 966
  pretender and, 127
  rulers and, 48, 937–38
  selfishness and, 851
  tyranny and, 938
  of United States, 769, 845*n*, 847*n*,
    1521
Nations. *See also* Country; National
    debt; Righteousness of nations
  British colonies and nationhood,
    xvi
  choice of government and, 1037
  Christianity and, 1160–62, 1196–97
  claims of dominion over another,
    637
  despotism and, 1013
  divine judgments on, 999
  divine providence and, 795
  God's conduct toward, 854
  God's destruction of, 796, 1335
  God's punishment of, 798
  God's sovereignty over, 612, 614,
    796–804
  honor and national union, 929

idolatry and, 980–81
independent status among, 638–39, 652
Jesus Christ and, 1052
law of nations, 1271
morality of, 795, 796, 804–6
national blessings, 1381
origin of, 642
power and, 640
religious perspective of nation-hood, xiii
righteousness of nations, 42–43, 567, 614–15, 647, 678, 804, 854, 965, 1214
rights of, 654–55
safety of, 1176
subjugation of neighbors and, 1137
young nations, 811

Native Americans. *See* Indians

Natural rights, 330, 351–52, 414, 444–45, 446

Nature. *See also* Laws of nature
defensive arms and, 725, 726
deistic maxim and, 1201*n*
following of, 486
God's operations and, 797
goodness and, 1208
infidelity and, 1192
Jesus Christ's sovereignty over, 200
mastery of, through reason, xx
self-preservation and, 263
as source of knowledge, 901
state of, 382, 388, 445
vice and, 1192

Nebuchadnezzar, king of Babylon
dream of, 187, 502, 805–6
God's pleading his cause and, 588, 592
invasion of Judea, 633
Jews' subjection to, 724

as tyrant, 694
wars of, 798

The Necessity of the Belief of Christianity (Edwards the Younger), 1187–1216

Neckar, Mr., 1245, 1291–92

Negroes. *See also* Africa and Africans; Slavery of Negroes; Slave trade
black complexion of, 1051
freedom of, 1508, 1509
instigations of, 599, 701
Jefferson and, 1457–59, 1508–10
origin of mankind and, 1457–59
Portugal and, 1041
race and, 1458–59, 1508–10

Nehemiah, 16, 590, 757

Nero (emperor of Rome)
Paul and, 723
prosperity of, 1335
subjection to, 722
tyranny and, 204, 691, 692, 694, 702, 1488

Netherlands
defensive arms and, 749, 1380
as free state, 482
French Revolution and, 1246, 1247, 1351, 1357
God's pleading his cause and, 594
New World and, 701
New York settlement and, 477
Portugal and, 1041
Protestants and, 502*n*
Protestants fleeing to, 455
religious liberty and, 750
rights of human nature and, 640
slave trade of, 1041*n*, 1042, 1046
strength of, 811
Tories and, 700
United States' alliance with, 786
United States' debts to, 938
William III and, 985

Neuwied, Germany, 1389

New Divinity, 440, 530, 884

New England. *See also* specific
   states
  Canada and, 477, 478
  charters of, 870
  Christian church in, 496, 512
  church practices of, 341*n*
  colonial ancestors of, 1546
  God on side of, 622
  government of, 168–77
  inspiration of, 1117
  militia of, 625*n*, 1140
  ministers' salaries and, 367
  morality of, 1561
  Patriots' Day observances in, xxiv
  persecution in, 365
  personal influence and, 1290
  presence of God and, 218
  Protestants in, 544, 544*n*
  Queen Ann's war and, 477
  religion and, 328, 962
  religious establishment in, 1086
  settlement of, 455
  slave population of, 1046

Newfoundland, 284, 478

New Hampshire
  convention of, 959*n*
  election sermons preached in,
    xxii, 942
  Evans's *Sermon Delivered at the
    Annual Election*, 1059–78
  Langdon's *Republic of the Israelites
    an Example to the American States*,
    943–67
  McClintock's *Sermon on Occasion of
    the Commencement of the New-
    Hampshire Constitution*, 791–813

Peabody's *Sermon Before the General
    Court of New Hampshire at the
    Annual Election*, 1323–38
  population breakdown of, 1045*n*
  slave population of, 1045*n*

New Haven, Connecticut
  charter of, 1092
  Dana's *African Slave Trade*, 1031–55
  Dwight's *Duty of Americans, at the
    Present Crisis*, 1365–94

New Historical Society, 1150

New Jersey, 730, 787, 1045*n*, 1086

New Jerusalem Church, 1572, 1576,
    1578–80, 1587, 1595

New Light (Side) ministers, xix, xx,
    52, 772, 1030

Newspapers. *See* Press, freedom of

New Testament. *See* Gospel; Jesus
    Christ; Scriptures; other New
    Testament figures; and Biblical
    Citation Index

Newton, Isaac, 893, 896, 897, 898,
    899, 1506–7

New World. *See* Colonial America;
    Spanish America

New York
  American Revolution battles of,
    781, 787
  devastation in, 625*n*
  Mason's *Voice of Warning to
    Christians*, 1449–76
  Miller's *Sermon on the Anniversary of
    the Independence of America*,
    1151–67
  ministers' salaries and, 367
  population breakdown of, 1045*n*
  religious establishment and, 1086
  settlement of, 477
  Sherwood's *Church's Flight into the
    Wilderness: An Address on the
    Times*, 485–527

slave population of, 1045*n*
suspension of assembly, 280
Webster's *Revolution in France,*
1237–99
Wortman's *Solemn Address to
Christians and Patriots,* 1479–1528

New York Bible Society, 1150

New York Democratic Society, 1478

Nicholas V, 1038, 1039

Nightingale, Joseph, 1174*n*

Nimrod, 19, 895

Nineveh, 27–50, 567, 856, 892

Nineveh's Repentance and Deliverance
(Sewall), 27–50

Nisbet, John, 1150

Noah, 203, 228, 593, 893, 895, 1510

Nonconformists, 346, 1083, 1087, 1094

Non-resistance doctrine, 396, 512,
732, 811, 1021

Norfolk, 625*n*

Normandy, 454

North, Frederick, second earl of
Guilford, 489, 704–7, 720, 758,
1022*n*

North America, discovery of, 454.
See also Colonial America

North Carolina, 309, 328, 1046*n*

North Sea, 984

Northwest territory, 1046*n*

Norway, 1505

Nova Scotia, 477–78

Nursing fathers of the Church, 125,
346, 861, 1091, 1471

Obedience
allegiance and, 452
British army and navy and, 779
to British Crown, 286
to British Parliament, 454
children and, 1360–61
dignity of man and, 893
to duty, 1318
to God, xx, 564, 585, 618–20, 810–11
to government, 80, 740–41, 877
Israel's worship and, 949
Jacobin Society and, 1360–61
Jesus Christ and, 37–38, 1071
of Jews, 612–14, 618
liberty and, 1071
of magistrates, 1016–17
to magistrates, 741, 922, 1116, 1430,
1432
to moral law, 948
national happiness and, 873–78
passive obedience doctrine, 396,
512, 811, 1021
personal, 1377
religion as voluntary obedience to
God, 347
to rulers, 921, 1070–71, 1360, 1431,
1443
scriptures and, 1378
servants and, 1360–61, 1431
of subjects, 922
war and, 489
Obedience to laws
British laws, 271, 281, 285–86
citizens and, 1070–71, 1496
civil officers and, 1070
disobedience and, 1084
divine judgments and, 1444
equality and, 1312*n*
golden rule and, 1158
government and, 961
happiness and, 1067
to laws of rulers, 387, 467–69,
488
liberty and, 1319
minister's support of, 1117
to moral law, 948

Obedience to laws, *continued*
  patriotism and, 1016, 1025
  religion and, 1108
  republican government and, 1320,
    1327
  rulers and, 1067, 1070, 1424
Objects, lack of soul, 889
Octavianus, 1204
Old Light (Side) ministers, xix, 52,
  1030
Old Testament. *See* Prophets and
  prophecies; Scriptures; names
  of Old Testament figures; and
  Biblical Citation Index
Olney, Jeremiah, 1174*n*
Olympic games, 1259
Omnipotence
  of France's national sovereignty,
    1253, 1254
  of God, 591–93, 662, 862, 979, 1013,
    1315, 1319
Omnipresence of God, 979, 1328
Omniscience of God, 978–79, 1191,
  1319, 1338
On the Evils of a Weak Government
  (Smalley), 1417–46
Ophir, 936
Oppression. *See also* Despotism;
    Tyranny
  absolute government and, 871
  Babylon and, 193
  benevolence and, 1158–59
  of Boston, Massachusetts, 743,
    756, 758, 799*n*
  of British army and navy, 622, 654
  as cause for independence, 638
  Christianity and, 1156, 1158, 1163
  of colonial America, 317, 603
  courts and, 1442
  duty to relieve oppressed, 764

  God's will and, 541
  gospel and, 1310
  government and, 1427–30
  individuals and, 1427–30, 1440,
    1442
  of Israel, 631, 1419
  laws and, 1427
  liberty and, xix, 305, 306
  lusts of men and, 662
  magistrates' authority and, 724
  military forces and, 872
  monarchy and, 1562
  people of God delivering them-
    selves from, 764
  of religious establishments, 1092
  rights and, 312, 377
  role in revolutions, 665–66
  scriptures and, 738
  of subjects, 735
  superstition and, 1161
  turned on oppressor, 679
  United States government provi-
    sions for removal of, 872, 874
Orange, prince of
  William III as, 130, 596, 870, 970,
    985, 993
  William the Silent as, 594, 749
*An Oration in Commemoration of the
  Anniversary of American
  Independence* (Emerson), 1557–69
*An Oration in Commemoration of the
  Independence of the United States
  of America* (Hitchcock), 1171–83
An Oration upon the Beauties of Liberty
  (Allen), 303–25
Order
  biblical image of, xv
  Christianity and, 1183
  government and, 13, 18, 142–43, 378
  mankind's general good, 145
  public order, 1107–11, 1118

ruling power and, 142–45
tyranny and, 167
war and, 572
Original sin doctrine, 538–39n
Osgood, David
biographical information on, 1218, 1220
Wonderful Works of God Are to Be Remembered, 1219–34
Othniel, 751
Ottoman empire, 809, 1083
Overcoming Evil with Good (Griswold), 1531–54

Pagans and paganism. *See also* Heathens; Idolatry
in Africa, 1051
Christianity and, 519, 990, 1194–96, 1485
as civil officers, 1098
Constantine the Great and, 1088
gods of, 1422
liberty and, 1160
Portugal and, 1039
religious liberty and, 1083
right of private judgment and, 1090
Roman Catholic Church and, 1257–58
temperance and, 1199–1200
United States and, 1191
Paine, Thomas, 494, 1008, 1473, 1474n, 1487
Paley, William, 1493
Pallas, 1205
Pantheon, 1262
Paper money. *See* Money
Papists. *See* Popes; Roman Catholic Church
Pardon. *See* Forgiveness

Parents. *See also* Children; Youth
children's honoring of, 1432
children's prayer for, 1353
children's subjection to, 445n, 452–53, 1430, 1432
Christianity and, 1114
civil officers as, 1070
dignity of man and, 905–6
religious education and, 1073, 1379
Paris, 1265, 1296, 1347
Paris peace treaty of 1783, xvi, 530
Parker, Matthew, 95
Parliament. *See* British House of Commons; British House of Lords; British Parliament
Parma, duchess of, 676
Party spirit. *See* Political parties
Passions of men
American Revolution and, 1285
Christianity and, 1310
constitutions and, 1299
fear of God and, 1328
French Revolution and, 1297–98, 1358
God's wisdom and, 674–75
government and, 1325, 1333
political parties and, 1285–86, 1294
praise of God and, 534–35
religion and, 1268
suppression of, 674
Witherspoon's *Dominion of Providence over the Passions of Men*, 531–58
wrath of men and, 535–44
Passive obedience doctrine, 396, 512, 811, 1021
Patrick, Saint, 1359

Patriotism. *See also* Citizens and
    citizenship
  American Revolution and, 850,
    874
  anarchy and, 1320
  children's education and, 1442
  Christianity and, 1011, 1166
  church-state relations and, 1118,
    1490
  of colonial militia, 679, 779
  conscience and, 931
  Cooper's *Sermon on the Day of the
    Commencement of the Constitution,*
    629–56
  duty and, 1482, 1498–1527
  enemies and, 1019–20
  of French Revolution, 1243
  Great Britain and, 1026
  Jacobin Society and, 1296
  Jesus Christ and, 1011, 1025–26
  just and reasonable, 1012–13
  justice and, 1012
  liberty and, 1013, 1015–16, 1025, 1026,
    1075
  men of ambition and, 1230
  mistakes in, 1009–11
  morality and, 1024–25
  national happiness and, 1153
  national prejudices and, 1276
  need for, 849–52
  obedience to laws and, 1025
  passion and, 674
  patriot cause and, 26
  patriotic spirit and, 378, 782
  Paul and, 1026
  of people, 1125
  prayer and, 1020, 1025, 1117
  Price's *Discourse on the Love of Our
    Country,* 1005–28
  representation and, 1024
  republican government and, 1319,
    1320

  righteous, 440
  rivalry and, 1010
  Roman Catholic Church and, 1358
  societies and, 1233
  sovereignty of the people and,
    645
  United States Constitution and,
    1482
  virtue and, 1013, 1014–15, 1025
  wrath of Great Britain and, 673
Patriots' Day observances
  Battle of Lexington and, xxiv
  Cushing's *Divine Judgments upon
    Tyrants,* 609–26
Patroclus, 1205
Paul
  atheism and, 894
  dignity of man and, 895
  fruit of love and, 827
  Galatians and, 1062
  Greeks' unknown god statue and,
    1259
  heathens and, 1201
  honoring dead and, 1403
  human inventions and, 829
  Jesus Christ and, 189, 1583
  Jewish converts and, 1033
  Jews and, 1026
  noble actions and, 893
  origin of mankind and, 1459
  patriotism and, 1026
  persecution and, 198, 204
  persuaded in own mind and, 830
  quoted, 1573
  respect for rulers and, 922–23
  Roman Catholic Church and, 499
  as Roman citizen, 158
  sin and, 526
  as soldier of Jesus Christ, 196
  subjection to magistrates and,
    722–23

Thessalonians and, 1591–94
Timothy and, 820, 821
war and, 574
wisdom and, 859
Paulus, 746
Peabody, Stephen
  biographical information on, 1322
  *Sermon Before the General Court of
    New Hampshire at the Annual
    Election*, 1323–38
Peace
  American Revolution contrasted
    with, 1335
  atheism and, 1462
  Christianity and, 1183
  civil society/civil union and, 93,
    936
  connection with enemies and, 1384
  cultivation of, 811
  David and, 939–40
  divine providence and, 958
  Duffield's *Sermon Preached on a Day
    of Thanksgiving*, 773–88
  enthusiasm and, 1298
  fundamental laws and, 918
  government and, 1142
  gratitude to God for, 1346
  Great Britain's terms for, 676–77,
    707, 708
  insults to government and, 1345
  internal, 874–75, 879
  Jesus Christ and, 1432
  justice and, 162–63
  laws of nature and, 917
  liberty and, 651
  magistrates' promotion of, 934
  of Millenium, 1000
  negotiations for, 688
  political parties and, 1544–45
  prayer and, 1144
  preparations against invasion and,
    1135, 1139–41, 1147
  presence of God and, 215
  price of, 788
  promotion of, 1144–45
  public administration and, 919–21
  republican governments and, 1438
  treaties and, 708
  tyranny and, 167
  uniformity of practice in religion
    and, 92–94
  United States and, 688, 707, 717,
    998, 1144, 1437
  war preparations and, 1133–34
  in worship, 879–80
Pedobaptism
  in Ashfield, 353–54
  laws for, 339–40, 347, 348–49
  Massachusetts and, 344
  Moses Mather and, 440
  ministers of, 360–61, 368
  taxation and, 357
Pedro I (king of Castile), 748
Pedro III (king of Spain), 748
Pemaquid, 477
Penal laws, 389
Pennsylvania. *See also* Philadelphia,
    Pennsylvania
  charter of, 415–16, 420, 432
  manumission in, 1053
  population breakdown of, 1045n
  rebellion in, 1229
  religious establishment and, 1086
  slave population of, 1045n
Penuel, men of, 752
People. *See* Citizens and citizenship;
    Rulers, choice of; Sovereignty
    of the people
People's sovereignty. *See* Sovereignty
    of the people
Pepperel, Mr., 478
Pepperel, William, 122

Perfect law of freedom, xvi*n*

Perkins, Nathan, 1236

Perkins, William, xxi–xxii

Persecutions. *See also* Martyrs
  Alien and Sedition Acts, 1520
  Christianity and, 542, 842, 1159*n*,
    1197–99, 1489
  Church of England and, 1491
  colonial ancestors and, 1515–16
  exclusion of, 802
  false doctrine and, 1369
  in France, 1087
  heathens and, 197, 745–47, 1197–98
  hypocrisy and, 1490
  National Convention of France
    and, 1258, 1262–63
  by pagans, 1263
  of popes, 1263
  Protestants and Protestantism
    and, 502, 502*n*, 802, 1490–91
  Reformation and, 543
  religious establishments and, 1114
  religious liberty and, 991
  Roman Catholic Church and, 1343,
    1348–49, 1349*n*, 1371*n*
  by Roman Empire, 204, 1198, 1264
  toleration and, 1087, 1493, 1575
  United States government and,
    1182

Persepolis, 856

Persia and Persians
  Arabians and, 1050
  Greece and, 850
  laws of, 758, 1329
  Mohammedism in, 1392
  monarchies of, 193, 813, 1368

Peru, 594, 936, 982, 1313

Peter
  advent and, 1588
  chosen generation and, 586
  Cornelius and, 576

honoring king and, 251–52, 1019
  Jesus Christ as king and, 189
  Joel and, 1589
  luxuries avoided, 853
  persecution and, 204
  as pillar, 14
  pope as successor to, 1352–54, 1488
  sermons of, 1538
  sword and, 727–28
  tax and, 310
  walking on water, 200

Peter the hermit, 1261

Petitions
  of colonial America to Great
    Britain, 240, 241, 248, 260–61,
    708, 720, 799
  failure of, 721, 1563
  governmental influence and, 871
  magistrates hearing of, 931

Phaeton, 126

Pharaoh. *See also* Egypt and
    Egyptians
  dignity of man and, 895
  divine judgments on, 982
  divine providence and, 593, 594
  first-born of Egypt and, 974
  God pleading cause to, 590
  God's omnipotent spirit and, 592
  Israel and, 777, 973, 974, 1476
  Red Sea and, 975–77, 981
  wrath of men and, 663

Pharisees, 81, 1543

Philadelphia, Pennsylvania. *See also*
    Pennsylvania
  American Revolution battles of,
    781
  Cobbett and, 1526*n*
  Duffield's *Sermon Preached on a Day
    of Thanksgiving*, 773–88
  Whitefield's *Britain's Mercies and
    Britain's Duties*, 121–36

Witherspoon's *Dominion of Providence over the Passions of Men*, 531–58

Philanthropy, 1036, 1054, 1176, 1182, 1540

Philip, 1257, 1526, 1583

Philip II (king of France), 750

Philip II (king of Spain), 594, 640, 676, 982–85, 1161*n*

Philip of Macedon, 1401

Philippics, 1498

Philistia, 593

Philistines, 754, 1403

Philological Society of Manchester, England, 1150

Philosophical religion, 1191, 1192–93, 1207–11

Philosophists, 1372, 1373, 1373*n*, 1384, 1388, 1390

Philosophy and philosophers
    advances in, 891
    boundaries of human knowledge and, 897
    clergy as philosophers, xiv
    conflict and, 1497
    of Greece, 1255, 1261–62, 1270
    heathen, 1438
    infidelity and, 1566
    Jacobin Society and, 1257
    knowledge and, 1133
    literary men as philosophers, 1251
    Locke as philosopher, 1312
    miracles and, 1503, 1503*n*, 1504
    morality and, 1318
    origin of man and, 1505
    philosophical morality, 1108
    religion and, 1107–8, 1533
    republican government and, 1267–68
    suicide and, 1206

Phinehaz, 636

Phips, Sir William, 477

Pickering, Mr., 1522, 1523

Pied Mont, 747, 748

Piety
    Christianity and, 1192
    church-state relations, 1122
    education of children and, 918
    happiness and, 1211
    of Hezekiah, 1379
    Holy Spirit and, 855
    liberty and, 1111
    of magistrates, 1115
    personal, 1377
    public order and, 1111
    of United States President, 1125
    Washington and, 1409
    youth and, 906

Pigott, Charles, 1474, 1474*n*

Pike, Leonard, 355

Pilate (Roman governor), 184–86, 189, 729

Pillars
    as architectural metaphor, 12, 14
    belonging to God, 17–19
    Colman's *Government the Pillar of the Earth*, 9–24
    Jesus Christ as pillar, 14, 23
    magistrates as, 21–22
    ministers as, 14
    as ornament, 14–15
    religion as pillar of government, 22
    rulers as, 13–17, 19–20, 22–24

Pinckney, Charles C.
    John Adams and, 1521–22*n*
    aristocracy and, 1495
    British party and, 1498, 1501, 1528
    Federalists and, 1521, 1523
    Linn and, 1481

Pinckney, Charles C., *continued*
  political freedom and, 1500
  political party of, 1483, 1521–24
  as presidential candidate, 1494,
    1495, 1497–98, 1522, 1525, 1525n,
    1526
  United States Constitution and,
    1524
  XYZ affair and, 1340
Pinckney, T., 1522
Pitt, William
  Dissenters and, 1022–23n
  Mayhew and, 232, 235–37, 250n,
    255, 256n
  Price and, 567
  as support of colonial America,
    276, 476, 601–2, 642
Pius VI, 1353
Plagues, 973–75, 1382, 1384, 1385, 1393
Plantations. *See also* Colonial
    America
  advantage of, 514
  charters compared to, 402
  dependency of, 279
  laws of, 466
  liberty and, 26
  ministers and, 341–42
  Plymouth Company and, 455
  rights of, 240
  Stamp Act and, 239
  taxation and, 277
  worship and, 349–50
Plato
  civil liberty and, 258
  dignity of man and, 895
  education and, 1204
  forgiveness and, 1202
  as philosopher, 134, 854, 1255
  truth and, 1201
  vice and, 1201n
Plutarch, 1200n, 1201

Plymouth Company, 455
Poland, 205, 1180, 1246, 1271, 1371, 1393
Political parties. *See also* Factions;
    Societies
  abuse and, 1543–44
  avoidance of, 964, 966, 1214, 1526
  badges of, 1285
  civil wars and, 1536
  factions and, 928, 937, 960, 1227–28,
    1271, 1273, 1534
  French Revolution and, 1239, 1266,
    1269–70, 1272
  government and, 1298
  happiness and, 1274
  maxims of, 1535
  ministers and, 1481, 1489, 1494
  opposition to United States gov-
    ernment and, 1229
  outrages of, 1532
  party spirit and, 1233–34, 1239,
    1273–74, 1540–41, 1547
  passions of men and, 1285–86, 1294
  peace and, 1544–45
  personal injuries and, 1273–74
  prejudice and, 1541–42
  private interests and, 1273–74
  religion and, 1275, 1466, 1481, 1532
  selfish purposes and, 965
  societies and, 1230–34
  speculative questions and, 1274
  tyranny and, 1273
  in United States, 1282n, 1534–36,
    1551
  United States Constitution and,
    1483, 1543
  United States President and, 1290,
    1520
  venom of, 1545–46
  violence and, 1275
Political sermons. *See* Sermons

Political slavery. *See* Colonial America as enslaved; Slavery as tyranny; Tyranny

Politics. *See also* Factions; Government; Political parties; and specific countries
   benevolence in, 1115
   in Europe, 1144, 1228
   Jesus Christ and, 1485
   magistrates and, 1107
   ministers and, 1485–86, 1492–94
   public religious instructors and, 1111
   religion and, 1108, 1121, 1452, 1465–66
   sermons as reflection of, xiv

Polonians, 749

Polytheism, 1461

Pompeius, 1281, 1399

Pontius Pilate, 993, 1052

Poor, Enoch, 1058

Popes. *See also* Roman Catholic Church; and names of specific popes
   calendar and, 1262
   claims of supremacy, 20
   defensive arms against, 747, 748
   Elizabeth I and, 983
   enthronization of, 715–16
   French Revolution and, 1352–54
   Italy and, 997
   kingdom of Jesus Christ and, 204
   persecutions of, 1263
   Portugal and, 1038–40
   power of, 499, 990
   Reformation from, 204–5
   religious establishment and, 1083
   revenues of, 1371
   right of private judgment and, 97–98
   See of Rome, 982, 985, 997, 1083

slavery and, 1038–39
tyranny of, 95, 197, 1268, 1488

Popular Party, 530

Porcupine, Peter, 1527, 1527*n*, 1528

Portugal
   Africa and, 1038, 1040, 1042
   antichristian secular powers and, 1371
   Brazil and, 1040–41
   French Revolution and, 1246, 1355
   Guinea and, 1038, 1039, 1040
   inquisition and, 1263
   Philip II and, 594
   popes and, 1038–40
   slave trade of, 1041*n*, 1042, 1046
   Spain and, 1040–41

Postelthwait, 1043

Post office, 469–70

Potipher, 593

Poverty, 875, 876, 879, 1112, 1202, 1423–24, 1437

Power. *See also* Omnipotence
   abuse of, 720, 740, 852
   arbitrary, 396, 597
   balance of, 487, 802, 1155, 1176–77, 1271, 1343–44
   of British Parliament to legislate for colonial America, 599, 691
   claims of divine right and, 632
   doctrine of, 512
   fiduciary, 737
   of God, 18, 382, 620, 662–63, 922
   of government, 58, 59, 79–80, 321, 339, 356, 456, 1515
   hereditary, 1435, 1519
   of Jesus Christ, 86
   justice in use of, 146–47, 165
   kingdom of Jesus Christ and, 729
   of kings, 321
   lawful, 723

Power, *continued*
  lust of, 992
  of magistrates, 737
  many with power over few, 346
  national, 640
  oppression and, 98–99
  people as right and foundation of,
      307–8
  religious liberty and, 95
  resistance and, 738
  of Roman Catholic Church, 990
  of rulers, 142–45, 1333
  temptations of, 859
  unlimited, 1072
  war and, 1137
Powers, Nicholas, 361
Pragola, 747
Prayer. *See also* Worship
  of children for parents, 1353
  church-state relations and, 1118
  days of prayer proclamations,
      xxiii, 1340
  as defensive arm of church, 729
  duty of, 1343
  for England, 1355
  fasting and, 35–36
  God's cause and, 591
  Holy Spirit and, 35
  Israel and, 945
  for magistrates, 935
  patriotism and, 1020, 1025, 1117
  peace and, 1144
  for pope, 1353
  presence of God and, 228, 229
  prosperity and, 854–55
  public welfare and, 1378
  reading prayerfully, 904
  resistance and, 729, 766–68
  role of, xix
  for rulers, 1471

  Sabbath and, 1381
  for soldiers of Jesus Christ, 196
  for success of gospel, 879
  Thayer's *Discourse Delivered at the
      Roman Catholic Church in Boston*,
      1341–61
  for United States President, 1345,
      1475
  war and, 563–65, 572, 576
Prejudices, 1276–77, 1541–42, 1595
Presbyterian church, 93, 530
The Presence of God with His People
      (Dunbar), 209–30
Press, freedom of, 986–87, 1347
Pretender
  Austrian Succession and, 125–27,
      129
  colonial America and, 243
  God and, 135
  liberty and, 396, 596
  Sullivan and, 130
Price, Dr., 563–69, 565*n*
Price, Richard
  biographical information on, 1006,
      1008
  *Discourse on the Love of Our
      Country*, 1005–28
Pride, 567, 828, 842–43, 1255, 1440,
      1445
Priestly, Dr., 1519*n*
Priestly, John, 970
Priestly, Joseph, 1006, 1572
Prin, Mr., 723
*The Principles of Civil Union and
      Happiness Considered and
      Recommended* (Goodrich), 911–40
Printing, 987, 1375
Private associations. *See* Societies
Private debts, 770, 1423–24

Private interests
  civil officers and, 1069, 1214
  evils of, 1010
  political parties and, 1273–74
  public interest and, 812, 1110, 1142,
    1143
Private judgment, right of. *See* Right
  of private judgment
Privileges. *See also* Rights
  choice of rulers and, 936, 1437
  justice and, 156–62
Procrustes, 1087, 1520
Procter, John, 363
Property
  aristocratical government and, 1083
  Boston and, 399
  children and, 1204
  civil society/civil union and, 429
  colonial America's cause and, 731
  connection with enemies and, 1384
  constitution and, 308, 398
  defense of, 57
  defense of country and, 1388–90
  defensive arms and, 1135
  distribution of, 492
  equal distribution of, 1175
  French Revolution and, 1250
  fundamental laws and, 918
  Glorious Revolution and, 986,
    1020
  government and, 58–59, 60
  Great Britain's infringement on,
    640
  Illuminati and, 1374
  increase in, 1337
  Israel's laws and, 948
  justice and, 1201–2
  law and, 1249, 1517
  as natural right, 445, 447
  parting with, to preserve rest, 1084
  plea in court and, 733

  poverty and, 875
  preserving of, 474, 1085
  public debt and, 845–46
  public faith and, 650
  Rhode Island and, 310
  Roman slaves as, 1203
  rulers and, 385
  security of, 848, 1178, 1344, 1410
  taxation and, 290–92, 297–98, 419,
    431, 447–48
  tyranny's invasion of, 923, 1061
  war and, 483
Prophets and prophecies. *See also*
  specific prophets
  of advent, 1587–88
  antichristian empires and, 1371, 1393
  chosen people of God and, 612–13,
    626
  of darkness, 1444–45
  defensive arms as duty and, 762
  false prophets, 1369–76
  God speaking through, 212
  of Isaiah, 1420
  Ishmael and, 1050
  Jesuits and, 1370
  Jesus Christ as, 186
  Jesus Christ as king and, 188
  to Jews, 795
  of Jews' government, 631–33
  of John, 497–98, 504–5
  of Millenium, 1000
  olive trees and, 1125
  Paul and, 1403
  as pillars, 14
  of righteous wars, 573–74
  Roman Catholic Church and, 499
  time periods of, 509–11
  use of, 869
Prosperity. *See also* Wealth
  adversity and, 1419
  balance of powers and, 1176

Prosperity, *continued*
  Christianity and, 842, 1189, 1206,
    1212, 1213
  civil rulers and, 859
  evils and, 839–53
  freedom and, 1061
  government and, 1142
  Israel and, 839, 946, 952, 1335
  justice in, 840
  luxury and, 852–53
  national, 540, 877, 1067–68,
    1378–79
  of Nero, 1335
  political, 1189, 1191, 1206, 1212, 1213,
    1410–11
  prayers and, 854–55
  presence of God and, 215
  of Protestants and Protestantism,
    842
  public prosperity, 1226
  religion and, 42–43, 853–54
  of soul, 894
  of United States, 839, 1334, 1337
  virtue and, 1332
  Wales's *Dangers of Our National
    Prosperity; and the Way to Avoid
    Them*, 839–63
  worldly, 880
Protection, 217, 452, 489
Protestant Dissenters, 1020, 1021, 1022,
  1022*n*, 1023
Protestant Reformation
  charity and, 826
  Christians' use of defensive arms,
    748
  colonial America's cause and, 603
  as fifth vial, 1370
  free inquiry and, 1515
  Henry VIII and, 134, 502–3, 526
  persecutions and, 543
  pope's supremacy and, 20

Protestants' fleeing to
  Netherlands and, 455
  religion of the gospel and, 24
  from Roman Catholic Church, 198,
    204–5, 338, 515
  scriptures and, 338, 1023*n*
  Spain and, 543
  tyranny and, 1161
Protestants and Protestantism. *See
  also* Christian Church; Church
  of England; and specific
  denominations
  in Austria, 749
  Calvinism and, 120, 208, 1023*n*, 1263
  cause of, 504
  charity and, 826
  charters and, 343–44
  choice of ministers and, 116
  Christians' use of defensive arms,
    748
  in Connecticut, 1092
  conversion experience and, xix
  divine commands and, 134
  double tax and, 295
  equal protection of, 644, 806
  in Europe, 205
  fleeing to colonial America, 544
  in France, 198, 515, 747, 750
  in Germany, 750
  governmental authority and, 21
  Great Awakening and, xvii
  laws of state and, 1097
  original sin doctrine and, 538*n*
  persecutions and, 502, 502*n*, 802,
    1490–91
  Philip II and, 982
  Plymouth Company and, 455
  preference of one denomination
    over another, 496, 989, 1097
  proselytizing and, 1054
  prosperity of, 842
  protection of, 352

Reformation and, 826
as remnant of woman's seed, 517
right of private judgment and, 55,
    75, 1090
Roman Catholic Church and, 1083,
    1198–99, 1293
second advent and, 1595
slavery of Negroes and, 1046
uniformity in practice of religion
    and, 91, 93
unity and, 648, 963–64, 1035
Williams's *Essential Rights and
    Liberties of Protestants*, 53–118
Providence, Rhode Island
Baptists of, 359–60, 367
Hitchcock's *Oration in
    Commemoration of the
    Independence of the United States
    of America*, 1171–83
problems of, 377
Provincial laws, 415–16
Prussia, 1246, 1267, 1271, 1392
Public administration. *See*
    Government
Public credit
of Great Britain, 649–50, 809–10
of United States, 650, 769–70, 1177,
    1247, 1564
Public days for remembrance, 1224
Public interests
private interests and, 812, 1110, 1142,
    1143
public order and, 1110
Punishment
of Babylon, 617
of chosen people of God, 615,
    1438
of Christianity, 1191
divine providence and, 670, 708
fear of, 393
fundamental laws and, 918

future state of existence and, 1192
from God, 218–19, 678–79, 795
government and, 59–60, 492
infidelity and, 1194
Israel and, 948
laws of God and, 611
of ministers, 106–11
of nations, 798
pardon and, 1210
proportioning to crime, 389
religious liberty and, 1063
rulers' role in, 1434
for sins, 1190
vice and, 1070, 1189–90, 1333, 1335
of wickedness, 917, 1210, 1223
wrath of men and, 666
Puritans, 96, 1161*n*, 1340
Pythagoras, 134, 1255
Pythian God, 1256

Quakers, 93, 729, 765, 816, 1136
Quebec, 477, 478
Quebec bill, 480, 514
Queen Ann's War, 477

Race. *See* Negroes; Indians
Ramsay, Mr., 1048*n*
Raynal, Abbé, 1043, 1252
Rea, 132
Reading, 901–4, 1243
Reason
authority of, 1191
church-state relations and, 1126
dominion of, 1027
enemies and, 1539
factions and, 1071
Festival of Reason, 1286–88
freedom of own will and, 56
government and, 143–45, 1176

Reason, *continued*
holiness and, 891–92
image of God and, 896
infidelity and, 1209
kings' statues and, 1261
knowledge and, 890, 1193
law of reason, 915
laws and, 1331
liberty and, 486
man blessed with, xix
mastery of nature through, xx
morality and, 1410
Notre Dame as temple of, 1253
religion and, 1251–52, 1310, 1317, 1533
religious liberty and, 1063
revolutions and, 1432
as rule and guide, 819
scriptures and, 134, 1587, 1593
theology and, 1581
true religion and, 1515
virtue and, 1191, 1337
as voice of God, 143
worship of, 1255–56
Rebellion. *See also* American
Revolution; French Revolution;
Revolutions
colonial America and, 310, 323, 489,
697, 722
connection with enemies and, 1384
cure for, 699
definition of, 308–9
kindling of, 691
of kings, 1017
Massachusetts and, 697
Paul and, 922
in Pennsylvania, 1229
republican governments
and, 1549
as sin, 722–23
suppression of, 675
tyrants and, 722
in United States, 1232*n*

Redemption. *See also* Salvation
doctrine of, 535–38
from domination, 1312
Holy Spirit and, 1055
Jesus Christ and, 192, 1534
Redman, John, 970
Red Sea, 593, 975–77, 981, 1420, 1436
Ree, 750
Reformation. *See also* Protestant
Reformation
personal, 1377
of religious establishments,
1014–15
right of private judgment and, 98
rulers' role in, 46
scriptures and, 1378
from sin, 38–40, 44–45, 1354
Rehoboam
authority of kings, 317, 323
cause from God, 671
God and, 668, 689
Israel's rebellion from, 722
lusts of men defeating own purposes, 664–65
taxation and, 321
tyranny of, 755, 955
Reid, Thomas, 530
Religion. *See also* Christian Church;
Christianity and Christians;
Church-state relations; Judaism;
Ministers; Protestants and
Protestantism; Roman Catholic
Church; True religion;
Worship; and names of specific
denominations
American Revolution and, 551–52,
600
atheism and, 1380
bible religion, 1087–88
bitterness and contrariety, 820

British Crown as head of church, 480

choice and, 810

choice of rulers and, 923

civil society/civil union and, 919–20, 923, 939, 1113, 1124

coercion and, 359

colonial America's cause and, 603

conduct and, 1115, 1117

conscience and, 1110–11

as cure for vice, 895, 1189

defensive arms and, 725, 728

despotism and, 1109

diffusing and maintaining of, 1111–14

dignity of man and, 893–95

divine providence as principle of, 793

duty to, 742–43

elections and, 1452

enemies of, 1489

executive branch and, 933

faith failing and, 823

French Revolution and, 1251–64, 1266, 1347–48, 1351, 1358

fundamental laws and, 918

God's chosen people and, 797

of gospel, 824

Henry VIII and, 74

Illuminati and, 1374, 1380

influence of, 1110–11, 1317–18

inward principle of, 166–68

irreligion and, 843, 906

of Israel, 945–46, 954–57, 962, 1419

Italy and, 1252

Jacobin Society's contempt for, 1291

kings and, 357n

knowledge compared to, 898

knowledge of, 1318

law of God and, 339

laws and, 339, 347, 356, 388, 1022, 1116

laws of nature and, 894

legal provisions for maintenance of, 1116

legislature and, 1120–21

liberty and, xiv, 1073–74, 1380–81, 1484

liberty of conscience and, 1121

magistrates' advancement of, 1116, 1119

manners and, 1566

Masons and, 1373

ministers' promotion of, 934

morality and, 966, 1268, 1410

national happiness and, 877–78

natural liberty and, 61–67

necessity of, for public order and happiness, 1107–11

obedience to laws and, 1108

as ornament of man's nature, 894

passions of men and, 1268

philosophical religion, 1191, 1192–93, 1207–11

philosophy and, 1107–8, 1533

as pillar of government, 22, 1126

political importance of, 1108

political parties and, 1275, 1466, 1481, 1532

political prosperity and, 1410–11

politics and, 1108, 1121, 1452, 1465–66

preservation of, 962–65, 1484–85, 1490

prevention of criminal actions and, 1109

prosperity and, 42–43, 853–54

public duties of, 1014

public interest of, 553–56

public spirit and, 913

purity of, 357–58

rational religion, 1320

as rational service, 1013

Religion, *continued*

  reason and, 1251–52, 1310, 1317, 1533

  republican principles and, 1572

  rulers and, 175–76, 760, 806–7, 1070, 1094, 1331–33

  rulers opposing, 760

  schisms of, 1093

  settlement of colonial America and, 455

  slavery as tyranny and, 1380

  submission to, 1117

  support of, 831

  Tappan's *Sermon for the Day of General Election*, 1103–27

  taxation and, 356–57

  tyranny and, 82, 91, 735, 1116, 1486*n*, 1517

  uniformity in, 91–97, 1089

  in United States, xiv, 1191

  United States Constitution and, 1098

  United States President and, 1465

  Virginia and, 1465

  virtue and, 915, 1074, 1109, 1111

  visionary men and, 826

  as voluntary obedience to God, 347

  war and, 566

  Washington and, 1405, 1408–9

Religious establishments. *See also* Church-state relations

  arguments against, 91–97

  authority and, 67–97, 966, 989–92, 1015

  causes of, 1088–91

  Church of England and, 1083, 1491

  civil liberties and, 1489

  evils of, 1087–88

  foreigners and, 1087, 1098

  Jefferson and, 1514

  Jesus Christ and, 1098–99

  knowledge of gospel and, 1091

  laws and, 347, 1083, 1092

  legislature and, 1093–94

  persecutions and, 1114

  reformation of, 1014–15

  religion standing without, 1086–87

  truth and, 1089–90

  United States and, 1098, 1114

Religious instruction and instructors, 1107, 1111–14, 1123

Religious liberty. *See also* Right of private judgment; Toleration

  ancestors fleeing for, 363, 508, 568, 872–73

  authority and, 67–69, 89–90

  Backus's *Appeal to the Public for Religious Liberty*, 329–68

  charters and charter rights and, 169

  of choice in churches, 99–102, 873

  church government and, 103–6

  civil liberties and, 549, 558, 734–35, 1495

  coercive measures and, 359

  colonial ancestors and, 363, 508, 568, 872–73, 1117

  in Connecticut, 1080

  conscience and, 740, 873, 1064

  constitutions and, 636, 644

  divine providence and, 1226–27

  in France, 997

  Glorious Revolution and, 988

  independence and, 417–18

  individual rights and, 99–102, 358–59

  Jesus Christ and, 1062

  justice and, 158–59, 169

  legality of, 1078

  liberty of conscience and, 362, 364–66

  loss of, 117–18

  magistrates and, 722

  in Massachusetts, 1080

ministers' salaries and, 347, 355,
  360–62
nature of, 1062–64
nonconformists and, 1083
oppression and, 305
persecutions and, 991
principles of, 1036
proselytizing and, 1054
Protestants and Protestantism
  and, 496, 644, 648, 802, 806
as right not favor, 1094
ritual of Moses and, 1034
tolerance and, 1490–91
tyranny and, 1061–62
United States and, 783, 783n, 833,
  872–73, 1440–41
Washington and, 1405

Religious tests, 1083, 1087, 1182

Religious toleration. *See* Toleration

Remand, Earl of, 748

Repentance
  dependence on God and, 879
  destruction and, 40–44
  divine judgments and, 39–40
  fasting and, 36–40
  God and, 31–32, 38–42, 523, 619, 795
  happiness and, 881
  Jesus Christ and, 45, 535–36
  of Jews, 797
  mortality and, 880
  national, 567–69
  pardon and, 1210
  Sewall's *Nineveh's Repentance and
    Deliverance* as, 26–50
  wrath of men and, 538–41

Representatives and representation
  British constitution and, 270–71,
    285, 1023–24
  British House of Commons and,
    1023–24
  British House of Lords and, 322

British Parliament's jurisdiction
  and, 468
choice of, 960
compensation for, 1084
delegates, 947, 1065, 1327
dependence on citizens and, 1435
election of, 1069–70
free government and, 490
laws and, 1066, 1084
legislative power and, 1065
liberty and, 1024
limitations of, 287–88
patriotism and, 1024
republican governments and, 1176,
  1319
Stamp Act and, 245
taxation and, 269–70, 280, 284, 285,
  288, 290, 292–94, 297–98, 356,
  363, 413, 422, 431–32, 447–48,
  1067–68

Republican government. *See also*
  Democracy; Free government
  advantages of, 1434–36
  colonial ancestors and, 1546–47
  delegates and, 947, 1327
  despotism of, 417–18
  French Revolution and, 1271
  Greece as, 1231
  grievances and, 936–37, 1435
  Israel as, 947, 955
  Jesus Christ and, 1547–48
  learning and, 900
  luxury and, 853
  men of ambition and, 1230–31
  monarchy versus, 1359
  obedience to laws and, 1320, 1327
  patriotism and, 1319, 1320
  Peabody's *Sermon Before the General
    Court of New Hampshire at the
    Annual Election*, 1323–38
  peace and, 1438
  philosophy and, 1267–68

Republican government, *continued*
  political orthodoxy of, xvi
  rebellion and, 1549
  religion and, 1572
  representation and, 1176, 1319
  Rome as, 1177, 1231
  slavery and, 1046
  sovereignty of the people and,
    959, 1176, 1177, 1215
  supporters of, 422, 436
  United States government as, 1177,
    1519
  virtue and, 811, 816, 921, 1102, 1125,
    1215, 1319–20
Republican party
  John Adams and, 1521
  faction and, 1547
  in France, 1241, 1253, 1295
  people's views and, 1243
*The Republic of the Israelites an
    Example to the American States*
    (Langdon), 943–67
Resistance. *See also* Defense and
    defensive arms
  of Christians, 745–50
  colonial America and, 1561
  constitutional right of, 736, 1021
  Continental Congress and, 799
  danger and, 732
  duty to, 721, 730, 741, 752, 758–59
  to evils, 727, 853, 1388
  fleeing from tyranny and, 740–41
  to government, 735–36, 738–39, 872
  grace and, 734–35
  to invading armies, 741–42
  to kings, 720–21, 731–32
  laws of nature and, 724–25, 734–35
  of magistrates, 737
  motives of, 742–43
  necessity of, 726
  neglecting duty of, 758–59

non-resistance doctrine, 396, 512,
    732, 811, 1021
  to oppression, 724–25, 923
  plea in court and, 733, 737–38
  power and, 738
  prayer and, 729, 766–68
  scriptures and, 750–68
  submission or, 799, 1388
  to tyranny, 721, 727, 752
  violence and, 729
Resolutions of Malden, 1130
Resumable power, doctrine of, 428
Resurrection, and death, 1401
Retaliation, law of, 522
Retribution, 1191, 1207
Reuben, 590, 592, 635, 636, 759
Revenue laws and equality, 1178
Revenue sources, 846, 1247, 1347, 1371,
    1560–61
Revolutionary War. *See* American
    Revolution
The Revolution in France (Webster),
    1237–99
Revolutions. *See also* American
    Revolution; French Revolution;
    Glorious Revolution
  Europe and, 1313
  experiments with, 1444
  government and, 1296, 1441
  Jesus Christ and, 1432
  oppression's role in, 665–66, 669
  Roman Catholic Church's stabili-
    ty amidst, 1354
Revolution Society, 1020
*Rex Portugalioe et Algarbiorum citra at
    ultra mare in Africa*, 1040
Reynolds, John, 1530
Rhode Island. *See also* Providence,
    Rhode Island

American Revolution battles of, 781

charters and charter rights of, 305, 309

Gaspee affair and, 306, 310, 312, 318

liberties and, 307

ministers' salaries and, 1094–95, 1094*n*, 1097

population breakdown of, 1045*n*

religious establishment and, 1086

Rhode Island College, 1406

Righteousness. *See also* Righteousness of nations; Virtue

advent and, 1582, 1585–86

British House of Lords and, 147

Canaan and, 567, 804

cause of God and, 584, 596

of citizens, 933, 965

civil society/civil union and, 916

colonial America's cause and, 603, 677–79

divine providence and, 1223

duty and, 585

eternal rules of, 386–87, 396–98

God and, 593, 860–61, 1013

Israel's worship and, 949

of Jews, 804

judges and, 227

laws and, 148

laws of Jesus Christ and, 743

of legislature, 933

magistrates and, 931

personal, 1377

of rulers, 146, 165, 175–76, 939, 1330

scriptures and, 1377

war and, 195, 573–74

Washington and, 1412

weakness in government and, 1446

Righteousness of nations

civil officers and, 1214

divine authority and, 647

divine judgments and, 804

morality and, 965

prosperity and, 42–43, 678, 854

sin and, 567, 614–15

Right of private judgment. *See also* Religious liberty

capacity for, 1090–91

choice of church and, 99–102

choice of ministers and, 115–17

Christianity and, 1054

civil power compared with, 356

government's protection of, 97–99

Jesus Christ's laws and, 84–87

liberty and, 55, 61–67

peace of Christian state and, 94–97, 1063

Protestants and, 55, 59, 75, 84–87, 1090

religion and, 1063

religious opinions, 1086, 1089, 1094

scriptures and, 72

worship and, 55, 90

Rights. *See also* Charters and charter rights; Freedom; Liberty; Religious liberty

American Revolution and, 1316

antecedent to charters or colonial constitutions, 445–56

attacks on, 481

benevolence and, 1159

British constitution and, 446–47

Christianity and, 1036, 1156, 1432

of civil society/civil union, 429, 456

colonial America as enslaved and, 443

colonial ancestors and, 1312

colonial constitutions and, 457

constitutional rights, 381

of countries, 1012, 1025

despotism and, 1075

Rights, *continued*
  duty to assert, 1311
  to free elections, 1065
  French Revolution and, 1164*n*, 1179, 1269
  government and, 445–51
  Great Britain's infringement of, 640
  happiness and, 1068
  of humanity, 429, 636, 640, 654, 922, 1315, 1561
  independence and, 1560
  of individuals, 99–102, 348–59, 931–32
  of Ireland, 654
  knowledge of, 1014
  laws of God and, 383
  natural rights, 351–52, 414, 430, 444–45, 446
  oppression and, 312, 377, 669
  of plantations, 240
  price of, 787–88
  restoration of, 1028
  tyranny and, 307, 923
  United States government and, 1061, 1177
  universal rights, 424, 437
  vice and, 1190
  vindication of, 1316
  Williams's *Essential Rights and Liberties of Protestants*, 53–118
Rights of conscience. *See* Liberty of conscience
The Rights of Conscience Inalienable (Leland), 1081–99
Rippon, Doctor, 1406*n*
Riswick, peace of, 477
Robespiere, Maximilien, 1259, 1270, 1286, 1295, 1497, 1566
Robins, 1520
Robison, 1376*n*, 1389

Rochambeau, Jean Baptiste, 782
Rochel, 750
Rollin, 363*n*
Roman Catholic Church. *See also* Popes
  ambitions of, 1487
  as anti-christian, 1355*n*
  beast and, 501–2, 502*n*, 525, 1368
  Belknap and, 1354*n*
  colonial America's cause and, 603
  destruction of, 515
  as dissenters, 1092, 1093, 1095
  doctrine of, 65, 1354*n*
  domination of, 1251
  double tax and, 289–90
  dragon and, 506
  Dunbar and, 208
  enemies of, 1354
  France and, 129, 135, 1252, 1371
  French Revolution and, 1244–45, 1251, 1269, 1348–50, 1358–59
  Glorious Revolution and, 1009
  governmental authority and, 20
  Great Britain and, 503
  heathens and, 1050
  Holy Spirit and, 1354*n*
  infallibility of, 1354*n*
  Irish Catholics and, 1359
  Jesus Christ and, 1354*n*
  kingdom of Jesus Christ and, 205
  laws of state and, 1096–97
  manslaughter and, 948
  Massachusetts and, 1359*n*
  morality of, 1354*n*
  pagan deities and, 1257–58
  persecution and, 197
  persecution of, 1343, 1348–49, 1349*n*, 1371*n*
  popish hierarchy, 1090
  popish plot, 126, 134, 396
  popish state, 91, 388

Portugal and, 1038
power of, 990
pretender and, 126–27
proselytizing and, 1054
Protestants and Protestantism
    and, 1083, 1198–99, 1293
Puritans and, 1340
Quebec bill and, 514
Reformation and, 198
Revelation of St. John and,
    498–99
Roman Catholic Society, 824n
scriptures and, 94
secularization of, 1371
slavery of Negroes and, 1046
spread of, 499–503, 543, 990
stability amidst revolutions, 1354
Thayer's *Discourse Delivered at the
    Roman Catholic Church in Boston*,
    1341–61
tyranny of, 1488
uniformity of practice in religion
    and, 93
United States government and,
    1359n
Voltaire and, 1372
Whore of Babylon and, 357n, 499,
    515, 1354–55n
William III and, 994
Roman Empire
    Arabians and, 1050
    aspirations of, 655
    Bartanes and, 746
    Christianity and, 519, 728, 1515
    Constantine the Great and, 1088
    emperors of, 184–85
    gladiators and, 1205–6
    Goths and, 1567
    Jesus Christ's kingdom and, 204
    laws of, 950
    oppression of, 193
    paganism and, 519

patriotism of, 1011
persecutions of, 204, 1198, 1264
race and, 1510
rise of, 813
rulers of, 723
Saturn and, 1258
slavery and, 1161–62
tyranny and, 392
Rome (ancient)
    Asian conquest of, 804
    assassinations of, 1204
    Catalinarian conspiracy and, 928
    Cato and, 1523
    character and, 921
    children's education and, 1442
    civil liberties of, 158
    destruction of, 1335
    factions and, 1280, 1281–83
    greatness of, 1552
    Hannibal and, 1086
    justice and, 1202
    knowledge and, 899
    laws of, 469, 1175, 1281
    learning and, 900
    liberty and, 1160n
    luxuries of Asia and, 853
    mankind's noble actions and, 892
    morality of, 804–5
    patriotism and, 645
    persecution and, 197
    philosophers of, 1255
    prosperity of, 856
    public spirit in, 808
    as republican government, 1177, 1231
    slavery in, 245, 1049, 1076, 1203,
        1204
    Sulla and Marius, 1281–83, 1297
    superstitions of, 1256
    vice and, 1197, 1199–1206
    virtue and, 811
    war and, 1202–3

Rousseau, Jean Jacques, 1252, 1489,
    1492, 1499*n*
Rule of faith and practice, 62–64,
    71–73, 75–76, 85–87, 94–98
Rulers. *See also* Kings; Monarchy;
    Rulers, choice of; Tyranny; and
    names of specific rulers
  accountability of, 384–85, 388, 1112,
    1121, 1157, 1214
  angels compared with, 15
  armed insurrections and, 872
  authority of, 20, 21, 1037, 1421, 1422
  benevolence of, 1332
  boundaries of, 146–47
  character of, 1334, 1424–25
  children as, 1422
  choice of, 851–52
  church government and, 71–72
  conduct of, 1425
  confidence in, 874, 1067
  conscience and, 176, 392
  constitution and, 146–47, 381
  cooperation from citizens and, 1386
  covetousness and, 1329
  divine judgments and, 33–36
  drinking and, 1425
  duty of, 805–7, 1070, 1327
  duty to, 863, 1433
  ecclesiastical rulers, 68, 70–71,
    1105–7, 1114–17, 1122, 1326
  election of, 871–72
  execution of laws and, 151–54,
    170–71
  as exemplary, 1333
  factions and, 922, 927–28
  fasting and, 45–50
  fear of God and, 166–68, 384–85,
    392–95, 1328, 1469
  God and, 1471
  golden rule and, 1158
  gratitude for, 1334
  happiness of, 391–92, 394

  hereditary, 1435
  infidelity and, 1469–71
  interests of, 1435
  of Jews, 338, 1105–6
  justice and, 145–66, 385–92
  knowledge and, 1331
  lawful, 723
  laws and, 386, 393, 488, 1084, 1330,
    1333
  liberty and, 1421
  licentiousness of, 1424
  ministers and, 1116–17, 1336–37
  as ministers of God, 806, 922, 1019,
    1070, 1422, 1433, 1469–70
  misconduct and, 1021
  morality of, 1424
  Moses as, 1106, 1326
  national debt and, 48, 937–38
  obedience to, 921, 1070–71, 1360, 1431,
    1443
  opposing religion, 760
  as pillars of earth, 13–17, 19–20,
    22–24
  power of, 142–45, 1333
  prayer for, 1471
  presence of God and, 223
  property and, 385
  prosperity and, 859
  public allowance of, 155–56
  public expense of, 1433–34
  public faith and, 650, 653
  public good and, 390–91
  punishment of evil doers and,
    1434
  qualifications of, 1327–29, 1422–23,
    1435
  qualities of, 919
  reformation role, 46
  religion and, 806–7, 1070, 1094,
    1211–12, 1331–33
  republican government and, 1435
  respect for, 921–23

righteousness of, 146, 165, 175–76, 939, 1330
Sabbath and, 1470–71
security and, 1430
selfishness of, 927
as servants of people, 1422
Sherwood's *Scriptural Instructions to Civil Rulers*, 375–407
sovereignty of the people and, 1157
spirit of Jesus Christ and, 1037
subjects and, 383, 921–22, 1435
trade and, 48
treasury and, 48
trust in, 391
truth and, 1328–29
virtue and, 646–48, 654, 807–9, 877, 1331–33
weakness of government and, 1422–25
wrongdoing of, 385–86, 390–91, 395
Rulers, choice of
elections and, 1327
fear of God and, 1469
Glorious Revolution and, 1021
and government, 401, 1426
and Moses, 920–21
as privilege, 936, 1437
religion and, 923
right of, 1561
rulers' qualifications and, 960, 1327–29
sovereignty of the people and, 959
Rush, Benjamin, 970, 1526n
Russia, 997, 1011, 1018, 1246, 1271

Sabbath
infidelity and, 1470–71
institution of, 1112–13, 1123, 1212
Jacobins' abolition of, 1253, 1258, 1350
Jefferson and, 1463–64, 1463n, 1470
Jews' observation of, 1392
observation of, 994, 1379–81
political, 1258, 1350
prostitution of, 1126
Sabe, 1041n
Sabin, Joseph, 1480
Sacrifice, 1205
Safety
God and, 214–20, 1379
government and, 143, 739–40, 1176
justice and, 162–63
public expenses and, 1434
St. Bartholomew massacre, 1293, 1294, 1488
St. Christophers, 1043n
St. Domingo, 1043n
St. John, Henry, First Viscount of Bolingbroke, 465, 1207
St. John's River, 477
St. Lawrence gulf, 478
St. Lucia, 1043n
Saints, 766–68, 892, 1257
Salaries of government, 401–2n. *See also* Ministers' salaries
Sallust, 1202
Salvation. *See also* Redemption
Christian ministry and, 934, 1124
doctrine of, 1462
evidences of, 826
gospel and, 923–24
Jesus Christ's suffering and, 200, 862, 890, 963, 1585
knowledge of, 987
necessities of, 825
of souls, 545–46
worship and, 878
Samael, 974
Samaritans, 200, 1011–12, 1036

Samson (Sampson), 17, 754, 811, 1403

Samuel
  Connecticut governor as, 858
  divine judgment and, 1335
  God's help and, 659
  Hannah and, 11
  Israel's government and, 1326
  Israel's king and, 636
  Jews and, 125, 135–36
  Paul and, 1403
  as pillar, 16
  scriptures and, 1594

Sanballat the Horonite, 757

Sandwich, John Montagu, 704, 706

Sanhedrin, 956

Saracens, 1247

Sarah, 1033

Sardinian monarchy, 1371, 1384, 1385, 1393

Satan. *See also* Beast; Dragon; Serpent
  apocalypse and, 999
  Christian church and, 518–19
  Dialogue Between the Devil, and George III, Tyrant of Britain, 689–710
  dragon and, 500, 509
  flood and, 511
  gentiles and, 1034
  hearts of men and, 828
  Jesus Christ and, 199, 1055
  kingdom of, 191, 501
  kingdom of Jesus Christ and, 729
  rescue from, 196
  tyranny of, 935, 994
  war of angels and, 506

Saturnalia, 1195, 1257–58

Saturn as pagan god, 1195, 1258

Saul
  David and, 727, 755, 766, 901, 1402–3, 1414n
  dignity of man and, 895
  divine providence and, 593
  honor of, 716
  as king, 316
  persecution of church and, 586, 587–88
  Philistines and, 754–55
  prayer resistance and, 767

Savoy, Duke of, 748

Saybrook platform, 1092

Scandinavia, 1257–58

Scepticism, 1126, 1223, 1251, 1492

Sciences
  advances in, 891, 899
  bitterness and contrariety, 820
  Chaldeans and, 891
  Christianity and, 1585
  church-state relations and, 1118, 1122
  dignity of man and, 897–98
  flourishing of, 803–4, 1337, 1575
  freedom of, 1181–82
  French Revolution and, 1250–51
  Greece and, 1016
  happiness and, 1071
  printing and, 987
  scriptures and, 1593
  societies and, 1279
  support of, 1077
  theology and, 1581
  United States government and, 649, 899–900, 1314
  Washington and, 1405

Scotland. *See also* Great Britain
  British Parliament and, 275, 282
  Church of England and, 1023
  constitution of, 273
  George III's tyranny and, 688
  heathens converted, 1392
  Illuminati and, 1376

laws of, 272, 274, 275
as part of Great Britain, 272, 289*n*
pretender and, 125–27, 129, 130, 135, 243, 396, 596
Protestant charity schools of, 127
rebels of, 395–96, 530
rule of, 126
Spanish Armada and, 985
subject to king but not to realm, 454
taxation and, 283–84, 289, 418
yule and, 1258

Scottish Common Sense philosophy, 530

Scriptural Instructions to Civil Rulers (Sherwood), 375–407

Scriptures. *See also* Gospel; Jesus Christ; Prophets and prophecies; names of Biblical figures; and Biblical Citation Index
abolition of slavery and, 1054
advent and, 1582
children's reading of New Testament, 1442
Christians and, 62, 74–76, 90, 1456, 1582
civil duties and, 1466
conscience and, 66, 1596
debt and, 770
defensive arms as duty and, 759–63
divine character and, 874
divine providence doctrine and, 533
doctrine of, 584
ecclesiastical constitution and, 1325
Fletcher's *Bible and the Sword*, 561–78
flood and, 1454–59, 1456*n*
form of government and, 1326–27

future state of existence and, 1209–10
God as first cause and, 798
government and, 76–77, 1431–33
happiness and, 1325
history of, 1133
humanity and, 1202
infidelity and, 1453–54, 1475–76
instruction and, 1133
interpretation of, 1090–91
Jefferson and, 1451–76, 1456*n*, 1465, 1503, 1504, 1506
judgments against tyranny, 598–99
laws of God and, 1476
laws of Jesus Christ and, 193–94
man's depravity and, 1429
ministers and, 1506
monarchy and, 1547
moral government of God and, 1207–9
morality and, 1105
New Jerusalem Church and, 1580
obedience and, 1378
oppression and, 738
order and, xv
origin of mankind and, 1457–59
pardon and, 1210
pedobaptism and, 339
personal reformation and, 1378
pride of man and, 547
Protestant Reformation and, 338, 1023*n*
reading of, 964
reason and, 134, 1587, 1593
as reflexive in meaning, xxi
resistance to evil and, 727
resistance to tyranny and, 750–68
righteousness and, 1377
Roman Catholic Church and, 94
as rule of faith and practice, 62–64, 71–73, 75–76, 85–87, 94–98

Scriptures, *continued*
  Samuel and, 1594
  sciences and, 1593
  scriptural meditation, xix
  sermon writing and, xxi–xxii
  Sherwood's *Scriptural Instructions to Civil Rulers*, 375–407
  sins and, 1377
  superstition and, 1581
  sword and, 561–78
  truth and, 1325
  unity of, xxi
  use of, 869
  Voltaire and, 1457
  worship and, 962
Scylla, 1229, 1259, 1526
Seabury, Samuel, 816
Sechem, 634
Secker, Archbishop, 1048
Second advent
  antichrist and, 999, 1393, 1590
  final judgment, 1191–92
  Hargrove's *Sermon on the Second Coming of Christ*, 1573–96
  millenium, 1000, 1353*n*
Second Awakening, xiii, xvii, 328, 1236. *See also* Great Awakening
Security
  civil rulers and, 1430
  distrust in government and, 875
  government and, 58, 60, 1142
  of happiness, 840–41
  of Laish, 1383
  personal security, 445
  preparations against invasion and, 1135, 1136
  of property, 848, 1178, 1344, 1410
  public security, 846
  religious liberty and, 1063
  sudden defense and, 1138–39

United States Constitution and, 1344
Sedition, 1229
Self-defense. *See* Defense and defensive arms
Selfishness, 851–52
Senate
  of Israel, 946, 952, 955
  Jefferson's farewell address to, 1553
  respectable members of, 803
  of Rome, 1281–82
  of Venice, 1176–77
Seneca, 134, 854, 1201
Senegal, 272, 1041*n*, 1047
Sennacherib (king of Assyria), 534, 666, 722
Separation of church and state. *See* Church-state relations
Sermon Before the General Court of New Hampshire at the Annual Election (Peabody), 1323–38
A Sermon Delivered at the Annual Election (Evans), 1059–78
A Sermon for the Day of General Election (Tappan), 1103–27
A Sermon on a Day Appointed for Publick Thanksgiving (Lathrop), 867–81
A Sermon on Occasion of the Commencement of the New-Hampshire Constitution (McClintock), 791–813
A Sermon on the Anniversary of the Independence of America (Miller), 1151–67
A Sermon on the Day of the Commencement of the Constitution (Cooper), 629–56
A Sermon on the Second Coming of Christ (Hargrove), 1573–96

A Sermon Preached at Lexington on the 19th of April (Cumings), 659–81

A Sermon Preached Before the Artillery Company (Thacher), 1131–47

A Sermon Preached on a Day of Thanksgiving (Duffield), 773–88

Sermons. *See also* specific sermons
  artillery sermons, xxiii
  Boston Massacre and, xxiv
  century sermons, xxiii
  convention sermons, xxiii
  election sermons, xii–xiii
  Fifth-day Lecture, xxiii
  Holy Spirit and, xxi
  Jefferson and, 1572
  newspaper reprints of, xxiv
  as pamphlets, xiii
  publishing of, xxii–xxiii
  as rhetorical form, xx–xxiv
  role of, xix
  steps in writing, xxi–xxii
  Thursday Lecture, xxiii

Serpent, 498, 509, 511–L12. *See also* Beast; Dragon; Satan

Servants, 737, 1037, 1360–61, 1431, 1432, 1433

Servetus, 1491

Sewall, Joseph
  biographical information on, 26
  Nineveh's Repentance and Deliverance, 27–50

Shadrach, 590

Shakespeare, William, 1513n, 1566n

Shaw, Elizabeth Smith, 1322

Shaw, William Smith, 1322

Sheba, queen of, 16, 722, 755

Shechem, 753

Shechemites, 216, 753, 953

Sheilds, Alexander, 712

Shem, 1510

Sherman, Roger, 1551

Sherwood, Samuel
  biographical information on, 374, 494
  Church's Flight into the Wilderness: An Address on the Times, 485–527
  Scriptural Instructions to Civil Rulers, 375–407

Shetharboznnai, 757

Shibboleth, 754

Shiloh, 954

Shinar, 892

Shipton, Clifford K., 1322

Sibthorp, 248

Siddim, 1378

Sidney, Algernon, 636n

Sidney, Sir Philip, 258, 639, 1014, 1311

Sierra Leona, 1041n

Silas, 158

Siloam, 1052

Simon Magus, 823

Sinai covenant, 1033, 1330

Sins. *See also* Repentance; Vice
  African slavery and, 1052
  as cause of calamity, 1354
  civil society/civil union and, 934–35
  colonial America's cause and, 677
  destruction of, 44
  divine providence and, 1452–53
  of enemies, 1382, 1393
  God permitting of, 659
  God's anger and, 403
  God's omnipotent spirit and, 593
  gospel-ministry and, 196
  Great Britain and, 567
  Jesus Christ and, 191–92, 963, 1035
  love and, 934–35

Sins, *continued*
  ministers' duty and, 1443
  of nations, 614–15
  original sin doctrine, 538*n*, 539*n*
  Paul and, 526
  prayer and, 1343
  public guilt and, 400
  punishment for, 795, 1190
  rebellion as, 722–23
  redemption doctrine and, 535
  reformation and, 38–40, 44–45, 1354
  repentance from, 36–38
  Satan and, 191
  scriptures and, 1377
  separation from God and, 42
  slavery as tyranny and, 333–34, 1077
  spiritual liberty and, 1154–55
  submission and, 332–33
  suffering and, 540
  trials and, 540
  of tyrants, 743
  United States and, 1438–39
Sisera, 593
Sixtus IV, 1040
Slavery and Egypt, 215, 507, 567, 635, 946, 950, 973, 1552
Slavery and Jews
  Canaanites and, 1050
  Egyptians and, 215, 507, 567, 635, 946, 950, 973
Slavery as tyranny. *See also* Colonial America as enslaved
  absolute government and, 805
  Christianity and, 1156, 1160
  free elections and, 1065
  French Revolution and, 1347, 1352
  government and, 427–28, 488
  Great Britain and, 240, 986, 994, 1027
  justice and, 1158

  knowledge and, 1071, 1155
  liberty and, 1027
  liberty of conscience and, 362
  oppression and, 1161
  religion and, 1380
  resistance and, 741–42
  sin and, 333–34, 1077
  superstition and, 1254
Slavery in Babylon, 1051
Slavery in Greece, 245, 1049, 1076, 1201
Slavery in Rome and Roman Empire, 245, 1049, 1161–62, 1203, 1204
Slavery of Negroes. *See also* Slave trade
  abolitionism and, 1049*n*, 1053, 1054, 1203
  Africa and, 1042, 1046, 1051, 1052, 1392, 1507–8
  Christianity and, 1046, 1048, 1049*n*, 1051, 1162*n*
  conditions of, 1047
  French Revolution and, 1350–51
  Great Britain and, 567, 641
  justice and, 1158
  Leland and, 1080
  manumission and, 1044, 1053
  mortality of, 1044, 1046
  passage from Africa and, 1046, 1047
  republican government and, 1046
  slaves' reaction to Stamp Act, 247, 251
  in United States, 1044, 1045–46*n*, 1046, 1053, 1203, 1392, 1507
  United States Constitution and, 1053
Slavery of the beast, 518
Slave trade
  abolition of, 1049*n*
  African slave history, 1038–47
  in Brazil, 1040–41

Christianity and, 1046
conditions of, 1047
Dana's *African Slave Trade,* 1031–55
Dutch and, 1041*n*
of Great Britain, 1041*n*, 1042–43, 1046
Leland and, 1080
popes and, 1038–39
Portugal and, 1040
in Senegal, 1041*n*

Sleep, interpretation of death as, 1259, 1376

Smalley, John
biographical information on, 1416
Emmons and, 884
On the Evils of a Weak Government, 1417–46

Smith, Adam, 1306

Smith, Chileab, 354–55

Smith, Chileab, Jr., 355

Smith, Dr., 1505

Smith, Ebenezer, 352–55, 353*n*

Smith, Elihu Hubbard, 1478

Smith, John B., 1462–63, 1511–14

Smith, Moses, 2nd, 355

Smith, William
biographical information on, 816
Sermon Preached Before a Convention of the Episcopal Church, 817–34
John Wesley and, 412, 419–20, 816

Smithfield, 1488

The Snare Broken (Mayhew), 233–64

Societies. *See also* Factions; Political parties; and names of specific societies
as aristocracies, 1233, 1279
factions and, 1230–34, 1277–78
in France, 1241–42, 1272
Illuminati and, 1375
influence and, 1279, 1289, 1291

liberty and, 1233
patriotism and, 1233
tyranny and, 1279
in United States, 1231, 1272, 1279–80
United States government and, 1231, 1272–73
Washington's death and, 1413

Society. *See* Civil society/civil union

Society for Promoting Christian Knowledge, 1130

Society for the Propagation of the Gospel Among the Indians, 1130

Society for the Propagation of the Gospel in Foreign Parts
Mayhew and, 232

Society for the Propagation of the Gospel in New England and Parts Adjacent, 8

Society of Cincinnati, 1170

Society of Jesuits, 1278, 1292

Socrates, 854, 895, 1182, 1198

Sodom, 567, 593, 751, 804, 842, 1201

Soldiers. *See* British army and navy; Colonial militia; Military forces; United States army

A Solemn Address to Christians and Patriots (Wortman), 1479–1528

Solomon
advent and, 1589
counsel of the Lord and, 659
dignity of man and, 887
fear of God and, 831–32
God's pleading his cause, 588
government appointment and, 152
happiness and, 892
history and, 1133
immortality of soul and, 888–89
Jeroboam and, 1423
justice and, 142, 149
knowledge and, 891, 906

Solomon, *continued*

laws and, 335
man's ruling over own spirit, 1431
noble actions and, 893
as pillar, 15, 23
presence of God and, 230
religion and, 895
on righteousness of nations, 678
as ruler of Israel, 187, 222, 316, 841,
    955
self-denial and, 557
subordination and, 1430
truth and, 1329
on tyranny, 395
wisdom of, 16, 18, 891, 904
Solon, 134, 950, 1201, 1292
Somers, Lord, 423, 426, 437–38
Somerset, New Jersey, 730
Son of God. See Jesus Christ
Soul
    Christianity and, 1432
    conformity to God's will, 828
    dignity of man and, 888–89
    education and, 905
    fasting and, 34–35
    immortality of, 1253
    nature of, 1584
    prosperity of, 894
South America, 1042, 1046
South Carolina, 410, 1044n, 1046n,
    1053
Southern states, 1083, 1099, 1225, 1507
Southwest territory, 1046n
Sovereigns. See Kings
Sovereignty of the people
    British constitution and, 308
    in choice of government, 645,
        808, 871, 1084
    choice of rulers and, 959
    constitution and, 653–54
    delegation of, 959

democracy and, 1177
forms of government and, 486–87
free government and, 808
Israel and, 635–36
legislation and, 1064–65, 1175
liberty and, 644–45, 1153
making peace or war and, 636
republican government and, 959,
    1176, 1177, 1215
rulers and, 1157
United States Constitution and,
    871, 1343–44, 1496
United States government and,
    1182, 1496
Spain
    adulation and, 1018
    antichristian empire and, 1371, 1393
    arbitrary government of, 424, 676
    Christian church and, 519
    Christians' defensive arms in, 748
    colonial America and, 255
    connection with enemies and, 1384
    divine providence and, 543–44
    Fenno and, 1524
    French Revolution and, 1246, 1355
    Great Britain and, 543, 597, 677,
        982–85, 1042
    inquisition and, 997, 1263, 1522n
    Netherlands and, 749, 1380
    patriotism of, 1011
    Philip II and, 594, 983
    Portugal and, 1040–41
    slave trade and, 1041n, 1042, 1044
    United States and, 651, 786, 938
    William II and, 134
Spanish America, 1040, 1042
Spanish Armada, 218, 970, 982–85
Sparta, 645, 808, 856, 950, 1200n,
    1202, 1203, 1335
Speech, freedom of, 60
Spirits, meaning of, 1368–69, 1444

Sprague, Ebenezer, 355
Sprague, Jonathan, 355
Sprague, Nehemiah, 355
Springfield, New Jersey, 730
Stamp Act of 1765
  British adoption of, xvi, 122
  colonial America and, 241, 244–49
  Evans and, 1061
  Mayhew's *Snare Broken*, 233–64
  Pitt and, 236
  plantations and, 239
  repeal of, 232, 239, 242, 246, 251,
    278, 283
  William Smith and, 816
  trade restrictions and, 512
  Zubly and, 266
State-church relations. *See* Church-
  state relations
State government
  civil officers' duties, 1329–30
  confederation of, 1227–28
  consolidation issue and, 1277
  constitutions of, 958, 998, 1098
  convention of, 930, 997–98
  factions of, 850
  Fenno and, 1524
  independence of, 1276
  interests of, 929
  jealousy between, 1276–77
  legislatures of, 1232, 1277
  people's vigilance over, 1231–32
  religious establishment and, 1098
  sovereignty of, 930, 1277
  subordination of, 1276
  United States Constitution and,
    998
  United States government and,
    1227–28
State religions. *See* Religious
  establishments

States, complaints in, 930
Steele, Sir Richard, 134
Stephen, Saint, 1403
Stewart, Dugald, 530
Stiles, Dr., 341*n*
Stiles, Ezra
  Dwight and, 1364
  Goodrich and, 910
  Hitchcock and, 1170
  Smalley and, 1416
  spirit of, 1551
  Thayer and, 1340
  Wales and, 836
  Williams and, 52
  Witherspoon and, 530
Stoicism, 1200, 1200*n*, 1201, 1202, 1206
Strong, Nathan, 884
Stuart, Moses, 1030
Stuart family, 396, 503, 703
Subjection. *See also* Despotism;
    Oppression; Submission and
    subordination; Tyranny
  absolute, 734
  defensive arms as duty and, 760–61
  to magistrates, 722–24
  passive, 724, 742–43, 767
  protection and, 452, 489
  to rulers, 921
  to tyranny, 759
Subjects. *See* Kings; Monarchy;
    Sovereignty of the people
Submission and subordination. *See
    also* Subjection
  to arbitrary government, 1053
  duty to, 1433
  to God, 143–44, 382, 554
  to government, 332, 334, 1126,
    1430–31, 1433–35
Submission and subordination,
    continued

to magistrates, 1019
pride and, 1440
to religion, 1117
resistance or, 799, 1388
sin and, 332–33
to taxation, 961
to unjust authority, 1334
of youth, 1360*n*

Succoth, 752, 1138

Suetonius, 189

Suffrage
  Christianity and, 1212, 1215–16, 1465
  of citizens, 645
  government security and, 1386
  liberty of conscience and, 1465–68
  of ministers, 1486
  right of, 1459–1550
  virtue of civil officers and, 1336
  weakness in government and, 1443

Sugar production, 1040, 1041, 1041*n*,
  1044

Suicide
  as heroic act of virtue, 1206
  as ruinous tendency in political
    view, 1206
  as vice of heathens, 1206

Sulla, 1204, 1281–83, 1297

Sullivan, 130

Sulpicius, 1281, 1282

Sunday. *See* Sabbath

Superstition
  bigotry and, 1181
  of Druids, 1287
  enthusiasm compared with,
    1254–61
  in France, 1252
  idolatry and, 1034, 1062
  Israel's worship and, 949
  National Convention of France
    and, 1258

oppression and, 1161
origin of, 1254
political slavery and, 1254
rational religion and, 1013
reason and, 1251
Rome and Roman Empire and,
  950, 1256
scriptures and, 1581
second advent and, 1590–91
toleration and, 1087

Surinam, 477

Swearing
  George III and, 695–96, 703
  practice of, 710

Sweden, 321, 749

Swedenborg, Emanuel, 1572, 1573, 1578

Switzerland
  antichristian empire and, 1371, 1393
  France and, 650–51
  as free state, 482
  French Revolution and, 1355, 1390
  Illuminati and, 1375
  liberty of, 640
  plagues of enemies and, 1384
  Swiss cantons, 594–95
  union and, 1385

Sword. *See* Defense and defensive
  arms; Military forces;
  Resistance; War

Sylla. *See* Sulla

Syria, 593

Syrianus, 746

Tacitus, 189, 1202, 1514

Tamerlane, 750, 1247

Tammany Society, 1151, 1154, 1478

Tappan, David
  biographical information on, 1102

Sermon for the Day of General Election, 1103–27

Tartars, 1050

Tatnai, 757

Taxation
British constitution and, 270, 284–86, 290, 291, 297, 419, 433, 447, 487
British Crown and, 284–87, 324
civil society/civil union and, 404–5
common debts and, 346
double tax, 280, 284, 289–90, 295
duties and, 285, 292
England and, 283–84
granting of, 286, 422, 429, 431, 433, 448
Ireland and, 284, 289–90
Jesus Christ and, 310
laws and, 287, 426, 918
luxury and, 1068
ministers' salaries and, 342–43, 343, 346–48, 352, 355, 366n, 368, 1097
partiality and, 283–84
public credit and, 769–70
public faith and, 650
Rehoboam and, 321
religion and, 347–48, 356–57, 363, 1092–93
right of, 253, 279, 281–82, 287–88, 292, 294, 295, 298, 353, 397n, 428
Roman Empire and, 289
Scotland and, 283–84, 289
selfishness and, 851
submission to, 961
types of, 282

Taxation of colonial America
British colonies compared with, 284, 418, 425

British Parliament's right of taxation, 253, 287–88, 292, 294, 353, 397n, 428
charters and charter rights and, 401
church-state relations and, 363–64, 368
colonial Americans as subjects and, 451
colonial assemblies and, 277–78, 291, 294–95
colonial Houses of Representatives and, 277
consent and, 290, 349, 413, 419, 447, 451, 480
Constitutional Answer to Wesley's Calm Address, 423–38
dependency and, 281–82, 295
to ease England of taxes, 434
Gaspee affair and, 310–11
independence and, 277, 290, 296, 419
representation and, 269–70, 280, 284, 285, 288, 290, 292–94, 297–98, 356, 363, 413, 422, 431–32, 447–48
revenue raising purpose of, 777
rights and privileges of English government and, 450
self-taxation, 430–31
Stamp Act and, 241, 246, 249
taxation without consent, 349
Wesley's *Calm Address to Our American Colonies*, 411–20

Temperance, 1159, 1199–1200, 1377, 1409

Temple, 40, 1262

Ten commandments, 584, 946

Tennent, Gilbert, 180

Tennessee, 328

Tertullus, 125

Test Laws, 1022, 1022n, 1023

Thaborites, 747

Thacher, Peter, 360
  biographical information on, 1130
  *Sermon Preached Before the Artillery
    Company*, 1131–47

Thanksgiving-day sermons
  Allen's *Oration upon the Beauties of
    Liberty*, 303–25
  Duffield's *Sermon Preached on a Day
    of Thanksgiving*, 773–88
  Lathrop's *Sermon on a Day
    Appointed for Publick
    Thanksgiving*, 867–81
  Madison's *Manifestations of the
    Beneficence of Divine Providence
    Towards America*, 1307–20
  Mayhew's *Snare Broken* as, 232–64
  Osgood's *Wonderful Works of God
    Are to Be Remembered*, 1219–34
  as sermon type, xxiii
  Whitefield's *Britain's Mercies and
    Britain's Duties*, 123–36

Thayer, John
  biographical information on, 1340,
    1342
  *Discourse Delivered at the Roman
    Catholic Church in Boston*, 1341–61

Thebans, 1204

Thebez, 753

Theocracy, 854, 1037, 1326

Theodosius, 746

Thessalonians, 1591–94

39 articles, 1083

Thomas, 1583

Thornton, John Wingate, xiii, 942

Thoulouse, 748

Thursday Lecture
  Colman's *Government as Pillar of
    the Earth*, 9–24

Keteltas's *God Arising and Pleading
    His People's Cause*, 581–605
  as sermon type, xxiii

Tiberius (emperor of Rome), 185,
    933

Time, 509–11, 527

Timothy, 820, 821

Tindal, William, 83, 1465, 1487, 1492

Titles of rank, 1269

Titles of respect, 1259–60

Tobacco production, 1041*n*

Tobiah, 757

Tocqueville, Alexis de, xiv

Toland, 1465

Toleration. *See also* Religious liberty
  British Parliament and, 1022*n*,
    1023*n*
  Church of England and, 1022*n*
  civil liberties and, 1490–91
  Frederic II and, 1465
  Glorious Revolution and, 1022
  gospel and, 1515
  infidelity and, 1490, 1493
  of nonconformists, 1087
  persecutions and, 1087, 1493, 1575
  United States and, 1575

Toleration Acts, 52, 116–17

Tophet, 704

Tories
  arguments of, 757
  bribing of, 700, 701
  doctrine of, 739, 752
  Duffield and, 772
  Ephraimites and, 754
  grounds for war and, 725
  increase of, 697
  Moses Mather and, 440
  neglecting duty to resistance and,
    759

as political party, 1266
subjection and, 723
tyranny and, 710
view of colonial militia, 753
Wesley as, 422
Toulon, 1265
Townshend Acts, 266
Tracy, 1523
Trade and commerce
    Adams and, 699
    Africa and, 1040
    American Revolution effects on,
        600
    British Parliament and, 275, 1562
    Canada and, 477
    Cape of Good Hope and, 1040
    of colonial America, 243, 317, 400,
        425, 435
    colonial constitutions and, 458
    duties and, 285, 292, 295, 324, 461,
        469
    encouragement of, 1564
    extension of, 1178
    fishing and, 1225–26, 1226
    free trade, 490, 516
    French Revolution and, 1239, 1250,
        1347, 1356
    fur, 478
    of Great Britain, 240, 242,
        479–80, 1521
    independence and, 638, 1560
    justice and, 163, 172
    of Laish, 1134
    laws and, 149
    liberty and, 490, 516
    of Nova Scotia, 478
    plantations and, 514
    of Portugal, 1040, 1041
    protection of, 476–77, 479–80
    public expenses and, 1434
    regulations of, 284–85, 469

    restrictions of, 512–13
    rulers and, 48
    Stamp Act and, 249, 251, 255
    taxation and, 291
    treaties and, 708
    United States' advantages in,
        869–70
    United States government and,
        1228
    United States' territory and,
        1174–75
    Washington and, 1405
    West Indies and, 479
Trajan, 1206
Treason
    civil rulers and, 378–80
    defense and, 463–64
    French Revolution and, 1242, 1270
    Gaspee affair and, 306
    Jacobin Society and, 1293–97
    judges and, 1520
    liberty and, 1297
Treaties
    Breda, treaty at, 477
    between France and United
        States, 1356
    between Great Britain and colo-
        nial America, 491–92
    between Great Britain and United
        States, 1521
    justice and, 163
    Paris peace treaty of 1783, xvi, 530
    peace and, xvi, 478, 530, 708
    Peace of Utrecht, 478
    public faith and, 809–10
Trenton, New Jersey, 787
·Tresilian, 1486n
Treves, Bishop of, 1389
Trial by jury
    Gaspee affair and, 318
    Glorious Revolution and, 986

Trial by jury, *continued*
  government and, 492
  Magna Charta and, 428
  right of, 240, 318–19, 448–51, 480–81
Trials
  divine providence and, 572
  ministers and, 106–10
  sins and, 540
Tribes of Israel, 929, 946–47, 952, 954, 955, 999–1000
Trinity. *See* God; Holy Spirit; Jesus Christ
Troy and Trojans, 1205, 1442
True religion. *See also* Christian Church; Christianity and Christians; Church-state relations; Judaism; Ministers; Protestants and Protestantism; Roman Catholic Church; True religion; Worship
  atheism and, 895
  charity and, 895
  chosen people of God and, 797
  civil society/civil union and, 918
  conscience and, 1064
  divine providence and, 557–58, 1222
  honoring God and, 1073
  Jesus Christ and, 957
  justice and, 1253
  knowledge and, 1181
  legislatures and, 859
  love and, 895
  moral virtues and, 1253
  prosperity and, 42–43
  reason and, 1515
  virtue and, 853–54
  want of, 840
Trumbull, Jonathan, 702
Trumbull, Rev. Mr., 401

Truth
  acquisition of, 1580–81
  advent and, 1582, 1585–86
  aid of law for defense of, 1090
  cause of God and, 596
  Christianity's ceremonial rites and, 1114
  civil society/civil union and, 916
  colonial America's cause and, 603
  duty to, 742
  God and, 228, 1090
  of gospel, 1070, 1090, 1575
  heathens and, 1201
  liberty and, xx, xxiv
  maxims of, 1338
  party spirit and, 1274–75
  patriotism and, 1012–14
  reason and, 486
  religious establishment and, 1089–90
  right of private judgment and, 1063
  rulers and, 1328–29
  scriptures and, 584, 1325
Turgot, Anne Robert Jacques, 1014
Turkish empire and Turks
  adulation and, 1018
  Arabians and, 1050
  balance of power and, 1177
  as civil officers, 1098
  as dissenters, 1092, 1093, 1095
  Mohammedism in, 1392
  patriotism of, 1011
  right of private judgment and, 1090
  tyranny and, 392
  war and, 997
  weakening of, 999
Tuscany, 1371

Tyranny. *See also* Despotism; Oppression; Slavery as tyranny
anarchy and, 1428
antichrist and, 728
beast and, 504, 518
Boston and, 399
of Catholic Church, 338
chosen people of God and, 613–18
Christianity and, 1158, 1550
church-state relations and, 1114
civil liberties and, 1061–62
colonial America and, 425
as common cause of human race, 1359–60
conscience and, 1061
consent and, 474
constitutions and, 923, 959
corruption and, 1155
Cushing's *Divine Judgments upon Tyrants*, 609–26
dangers of, 392
defensive arms and, 717, 742
dragon and, 508–10
duty to resist, 721, 730, 741
Europe and, 1226
as extreme, 1334
factions and, 1294
fear and, 667
fear of God and, 167, 395
fleeing from, 740–41
of France, 1346
George III (king of England) as tyrant, 689–710
government and, 83, 429, 735–36
Great Britain and, 694, 720, 994
history and, 1075–76
invasion and, 870
Jesuits and, 512
judgment and, 726
judgments against, by God, 609–26

judgments against, in scriptures, 598–99
justice and, 147, 390
of kings, 730, 731
knowledge and, 1014, 1155
laws and, 148, 722, 735
laws of nature and, 59, 735
liberty and, 334, 392, 691, 986, 1071–72, 1313
liberty of conscience and, 362
Massachusetts and, 480
Micah and, 315
National Convention commissioners and, 1242
national debt and, 938
Nero and, 691, 692, 694, 702, 1488
oppression and, 305, 306, 386
Paul and, 922
personal, 1025
political parties and, 1273
of popes, 95, 197, 1268, 1488
power of, 740–41
prayer and, 729
prevention of, 1139
property and, 923, 1061
public injustice and, 848
rebellion and, 722
reformation and, 1161
religion and, 82, 91, 1116, 1486n, 1517
religious liberty and, 1061–62
religious revival and, xvii
religious tyranny, 1063–64
resistance against, 721, 727, 741–43
revolutions against, 665
rights and, 307, 923
Roman Catholic Church and, 501, 1408
of Satan, 935, 994
of sins, 1077
slave trade and, 1047
societies and, 1279
spiritual, 333

Tyranny, *continued*
  subjection to, 759
  taxation and, 433
  vice and, 1155
Tyrconel, Lord, 276

Union. *See* Civil society/civil union
Union Theological Seminary, 1448
Unitarianism, 232, 658, 1170
United Belgic provinces, 776
United Provinces, 1161*n*. *See also*
  Netherlands
United States
  abolition of slavery in, 1053
  allies of, 1076
United States, *continued*
  American Revolution commit-
    ment and, 651–52, 1358
  ancient maxims of, 1546–47,
    1550–51
  aristocracy and, 1289
  cause of, 1173
  Christian church in, 804
  Christianity and, 830, 831, 1166, 1392,
    1550–51
  civil liberties and, 783, 833, 1441
  classical rhetoric and, xxii
  compact and, 1083–84
  credit of, 650
  dignity among nations and, 958
  divine favor of, 787
  divine judgments and, 788, 1439
  Europe's political upheaval and,
    1299
  Europe's support for, 654, 693,
    698–99
  as example to Europe, 1314
  flattery concerning greatness of,
    855–56
  foreign attachments of, 1550

freedom of the press and, 987
French alliance of, 650–51, 675,
  693, 697, 746, 780–81, 785–86, 801
French liberty compared with,
  1497, 1566
French Revolution and, 1271, 1285,
  1355–58
frontiers of, 1145
gifts of nature, 840
as glorious empire, 833
God's help and, 782
as good land, 869–73
Great Britain's oppression uniting,
  670
Great Britain's relationship with,
  999, 1141
heathens converted, 1392
Illuminati and, 1376
infidelity and, 1438
internal enemies of, 672–73
Israel compared to, 631
Jacobin Society in, 1292
Jerusalem compared to, 913–14,
  1437
Jews of, 1392
Judah compared to, 1437
Langdon's *Republic of the Israelites
  an Example to the American States*,
  943–67
liberty and, 833, 1071, 1076
love of money and, 769–70
Madison's *Manifestations of the
  Beneficence of Divine Providence
  Towards America*, 1307–20
national debt of, 769, 845*n*, 847*n*,
  1521
national happiness and, 873–78
national prejudices of, 1276–77
as nation born, 776
natural advantages of, 1174–76
natural beauty of, 655, 1166
Netherlands alliance, 786

party spirit in, 1286
peace and, 688, 707, 717, 998, 1144, 1437
political parties in, 1282*n*, 1534–36, 1551
price of independence and, 860, 876
privileges of, 1437
prospects of, 1437–41
prosperity of, 839, 1334, 1337
rebellion in, 1232*n*
religion in, xiii, xiv, 1191
religious establishments and, 1114
religious liberty and, 783, 783*n*, 833, 872–73, 988–89, 1440–41
as rising nation, 701
security of, 1390
sins and, 1438–39
slavery of Negroes in, 1044, 1045–46*n*, 1046, 1053, 1203, 1392, 1507
slave trade and, 1042–46
societies in, 1231, 1272, 1279–80
Spain and, 651, 786, 938
spiritual revolution of, xvii
standing army of, 1267
state interests and, 929
territory of, 803, 869, 1174–76
toleration and, 1575
trade and commerce and, 869–70, 1174–75
treaties with French, 1356
treaties with Great Britain, 1521
union within, 811–12
as wilderness, 655, 1312
worship and, 1438
United States army, 652–53, 1232*n*. *See also* Colonial militia
United States Congress and religious establishment, 1098. *See also* Continental Congress

United States Constitution
Adams and, 1483, 1519–20
adoption of, 997–99
Backus and, 328
British constitution and, 998
British party and, 1527–28
Christianity and, 1500, 1525
church-state relations and, 1118, 1494
colonial ancestors and, 1547
constitutional convention and, 959
divine providence and, 957, 1436, 1484
elections and, 1498
enemies of, 1501
excellence of, 1177, 1334
Federalists and, 1523
God and, 1471–72
government reform and, 1273, 1566–67
gratitude to God for, 1165–66
Hamilton and, 1524, 1527
irreligion and, 1471–72
Jefferson and, 1483
liberty and, 871, 957, 972, 1061, 1343–44
liberty of conscience and, 1518
ministers and, 1525*n*
New Hampshire's acceptance of, 959*n*
Pinckney and, 1524
political parties hostile to, 1483, 1543
principles of, 1525–26
religious establishment and, 1098
religious tests and, 1182
safety of, 1536
security and, 1344
sovereignty of the people and, 871, 1343–44, 1496
support of, 966, 1145, 1543, 1564

United States Constitution, *continued*
  United States President and, 1483,
    1496
  Washington and, 1408
United States government. *See also*
  State government
  administration of, 876–77
  adoption of, 997–99
  arts and, 649, 899–900, 1314
  attainment of, 643
  balanced powers of, 802, 1176
  at beginning of American
    Revolution, 672
  burdens of, 936
  choice in form of, 801–2, 870
  citizens' agreement on, 914
  civil officers' duties, 1329–30
  divine providence and, 1334,
    1436–37
  duty to, 1343
United States government, *continued*
  education and, 648–49
  establishment of, 958, 967, 1314
  as example of free government,
    1126
  excellencies of, 1319
  expenditures of, 1067–68
  factions and, 1228, 1232, 1294
  French Revolution and, 1356, 1357*n*,
    1385
  gratitude for, 1227
  gratitude to God for, 1343–46
  insults to, 1345
  obedience to laws and, 1319
  opposition to, 1229, 1386
  party spirit and, 1277
  preservation of, 960, 1569
  principles of, 957
  public virtue and, 1182
  reform of, 1273
  religious establishment and, 1086

  removal of oppression and, 872,
    874
  as republican government, 1177, 1519
  rights and, 1061, 1177
  Roman Catholic Church and,
    1359*n*
  safety of, 1536
  sciences and, 649, 899–900, 1314
  societies and, 1231, 1272–73
  sovereignty of the people and,
    1182, 1496
  states and, 1227–28
  unnecessary expenses of, 937, 965
  virtue of governors, 646–47
  voluntary aid of individuals and,
    848
United States President
  aristocracy and, 1290
  choice of, 1344
  election of, 1453
  example of, 1125
  Fenno and, 1524
  infidelity and, 1452, 1468, 1474, 1476
  limitations on, 959
  Mason's *Voice of Warning to*
    Christians, 1449–76
  political parties and, 1290, 1520
  prayer for, 1345, 1475
  religion and, 1465
  United States Constitution and,
    1483, 1496
  Washington as, 1408, 1409
  Wortman's *Solemn Address to*
    Christians and Patriots, 1479–1528
Unity
  of Bible, xxi
  of faith, 91–97
  of persons, 16–17
Universalism, 970
Universities. *See* Colleges and universities; Education

Ursuline Convent, 1340
Utrecht, Peace of, 478
Uzzah, 756

Valenciennes, 749
Valentinian, 746
Vallens, 746
Vane, Henry, 342n
Van Hook, Mr., 1482
Vartorella, William F., 1238
La Vendee, 1292, 1294–95, 1347
Venice
    antichristian empire and, 1371, 1393
    balance of power and, 1176–77
    fall of, 811
    French Revolution and, 1352, 1357
    plagues of enemies and, 1384
    union and, 1385
Venus, 1195
Verecundia plebis, 921
Vermont, xxii, 1045n
Vice. *See also* Evils; Licentiousness;
    Sins
    avoidance of, 963
    Christians and, 1199–1206
    Christian states and, 1196
    civil officers' suppression of, 1070
    civil penalities and, 1189–91
    colonial militia and, 718
    discouragement of, 1014
    heathens and, 1199–1206
    hypocrisy as, 1519n
    influence of, 1213–14
    irreligion and, 1111
    Israel and, 955
    liberty and, 992
    magistrates restraining, 930–31, 1142
    motives to, 1193
    nature and, 1192

    paganism and, 1195
    patriotism and, 1025
    punishment of, 1189–90, 1333, 1335
    religion as cure for, 895, 1189
    restraint from, 1192, 1194
    rights and, 1190
    tyranny and, 1155
    wretchedness and, 873
Vid. Pool Synopsis, 756
Vidius Pollio, 1203
Violence, 729, 1066, 1089, 1135, 1164n,
    1275. *See also* Defense and defen-
    sive arms; War
Virgil, 410, 423, 1200
Virginia
    American Revolution battles of,
      781
    British constitution and, 460–61
    camp meetings and, 328
    Charles II and, 461–62
    Davies's *Mediatorial Kingdom and
      Glories of Jesus Christ*, 181–206
    insurrection in, 469
    Madison's *Manifestations of the
      Beneficence of Divine Providence
      Towards America*, 1307–20
    population breakdown of, 1046n
    Reformation in, 205
    religion and, 1465
    taxation and, 433
Virginia Companies, 455
Virgin Mary, 1257
Virtue. *See also* Benevolence;
    Charity; Duty; Faith; Gratitude;
    Honor; Industry; Love;
    Morality; Piety; Righteousness;
    Wisdom
    administration of government
      and, 877, 957
    Christian, 832, 1156, 1332, 1438
    of citizens, 877, 1337–38, 1435

Virtue, *continued*
of civil officers, 1069, 1070, 1116,
1120, 1122, 1335
civil society/civil union and,
919–20
conscience and, 1337
education of children and, 878, 918
elections and, 1125
enemies' capacity for, 1539
executive branch and, 933
free government and, 1333
God and, 873–74, 1317, 1318
government and, 1335
happiness and, 873–78, 1211, 1318
Illuminati and, 1374
irreligion and, 1320
laws of God and, 1318, 1320
liberty and, 1074
magistrates and, 1115, 1189
ministers and, 935
moral virtues, 163, 1253, 1280
motives and, 1192, 1193, 1194
national, 878
paper money and, 938–39
patriotism and, 1013, 1014–15, 1025
of people, 877, 1337–38, 1435
practice of, 853–54
private virtues, 1189, 1378
prosperity and, 1332
public order and, 1111
public virtue, 805, 807–9, 957, 1182
reason and, 1191, 1337
religion and, 915, 1074, 1109, 1111
republican government and, 811,
816, 921, 1102, 1125, 1215, 1319–20
rulers and, 646–48, 654, 807–9,
877, 1331–33
securing land by, 869
true religion and, 853–54
The Voice of Warning to Christians
(Mason), 1449–76
Volney, 1487, 1492

Voltaire
argument of infidels and, 1492
Christianity and, 1372–73, 1464,
1465
dangers of philosophy, 1383
flood and, 1503*n*
Jefferson and, 1455
liberty and, 1252
philosophism and, 1373*n*
quoted, 640*n*
religion and, 1487
scriptures and, 1457
Volusian, 715
Voting. *See* Elections; Suffrage

Waldenses, 204, 502*n*, 747–48
Waldo, 747
Wales, 272, 289. *See also* Great Britain
Wales, John, 836
Wales, Samuel
biographical information on, 836
*Dangers of Our National Prosperity;
and the Way to Avoid Them*, 837–63
Walker, Admiral, 477
Wallingford Controversy, 1030
Waloons. *See* Waldenses
War. *See also* American Revolution;
Defense and defensive arms;
French Revolution; Military
forces; Resistance; Revolutions
adopting other wars, 1144
in Africa, 1047
of angels, 506, 574
chosen people of God and, 613
Christianity and, 576
colonial America and, 235
in defense of virtue, 573
defensive, 1019, 1136–37
in Europe, 1228
fasting and, 563, 570, 572, 576–78

Federalists and, 1523
France's capability of sustaining, 1246
God and, 211–14, 571, 1137–38, 1376
with Indians, 477, 1230, 1232*n*
iniquity of, 1020
Jesus Christ and, 195, 572–73
justice and, 162–63
justification for, 725–26, 1050
kings and, 574–76
against lawful king, 724–25
liberty and, 483
lusts of men and, 662
to maintain order and justice, 572
morality and, 1265
offensive, 1019, 1077, 1246
power and, 1137
prayer and, 563–65, 572, 576
preparations for, 1133–34, 1147
private injuries and, 726–27
private versus public interest and, 1143
Quakers and, 729
religion and, 566
righteousness and, 195, 573–74
Romans and, 1202–3
slavery and, 1076
soldiers of Christ and, 624
wrath of men and, 537
wrongs sustained and, 725–26

Warren, Commodore, 478

Warren, Joseph, 653, 785

Warren, Mercy Otis, xiv

Washington, George
agriculture and, 1405, 1407
American Revolution and, 1407
character of, 1411–12, 1511, 1552, 1553
conduct of, 1404–5, 1407
confidence of people and, 1067
Cornwallis and, 703
days of prayer, fasting, and thanksgiving proclamations, xxiii
death of, xxiv, 1411
Defensive Arms Vindicated dedicated to, 715–17
degree of Doctor of Laws and, 1406*n*
divine judgments and, 1439
divine providence and, 958, 1391, 1405, 1407
education of, 1405
fear of God and, 1409
French leaders compared with, 1497
gratitude for, 1334, 1344
hand of God and, 784–85
Holcombe's *Sermon Occasioned by the Death of Washington*, 1397–1414
honoring of, 1568
influence of, 1289–90
inspiration from, 1569
Jefferson compared to, 1553*n*
Jews and, 1182*n*
as Joseph, xxiv
as Joshua, 784, 786
Leland and, 1080
liberty and, 1313
Matthias compared to, 745
morality and, 1405, 1408
noble actions and, 893
recalled as commander-in-chief of army, 1340, 1408
religion and, 1405, 1408–9
saving colonial America from enslavement, 745
service to country and, 1407–8
United States Constitution and, 1408
as United States President, 1408, 1409

Washington, George, *continued*
    worship and, 1469
    Yorktown and, 782
    youth of, 1406–7
Washington, D.C.
    Hargrove's *Sermon on the Second
        Coming of Christ*, 1573–96
Watson, Bishop, 1351
Wealth. *See also* Prosperity
    corruption and, 842
    obedience and, 873
    Sodom and, 842
    temptations of, 859
Weare, President, 802*n*
Webster, Daniel, 1218
Webster, Noah
    biographical information on, 1236,
        1238
    Revolution in France, 1237–99
Webster, Noah, Sr., 1236
Weeden, General, 782
Weishaupt, Adam, 1374
Wesley, Charles, xvii, 120, 410, 560
Wesley, John
    biographical information on, 410,
        412
    British constitution and, 427
    *Calm Address to Our American
        Colonies*, 411–20, 422
    Fletcher and, 560
    government and, 429
    Methodism and, xvii
    plagiarism and, 422, 424, 425, 432,
        434
    William Smith, 412, 419–20, 816
    voting and, 430
    Whitefield and, 120
    Winchester and, 970
West, 1030, 1493

West Indies
    antichristian empire and, 1393
    British West Indies, 1043
    Christian conversion of slaves
        and, 1048
    French Revolution and, 1350–51
    French West Indies, 1042–43, 1044
    health and, 1225
    Philip II and, 594
    slave population of, 1044, 1046
    slave trade and, 1042–46
    trade and, 479
Wharton, Rev. Mr. Charles Henry,
    824*n*
Wheelock, Eleazar, 328, 836, 1416
Whig, 1266
White, William, 368, 772
Whitefield, George
    biographical information on, 120,
        122
    *Britain's Mercies, and Britain's
        Duties*, 121–36
    Cumings and, 658
    Duffield and, 772
    Fletcher and, 560
    Methodism and, 410
    as New Light minister, xix
    religious revivalism and, xvii, xviii
    Sewall and, 26
    Thacher and, 1130
Whitgift, Archbishop of Canterbury,
    95–96
Whittelsey, Cathrine, 1030
Wickedness, 738, 917, 1210, 1223
Wickliffe, John, 83, 115–16, 204
Wickliffites, 1263
Wilderness
    Christian church and, 508–9, 522
    colonial America as, 503–4, 508,
        1117, 1546

industry and, 1178

Jews and, 1392, 1420

Sherwood's *Church's Flight into the Wilderness: An Address on the Times*, 485–527

United States as, 655, 1312

woman and, 506–8, 516

Wilkes, John, 302, 424

William, Duke, 130

William I (king of England), 124, 420, 437, 454

William III (king of England)
Glorious Revolution of, xxiii, 96, 134, 395, 639, 870, 970, 985

James II and, 130, 596

Jesus Christ compared to, 992–95

liberty of conscience and, 988

power of, 38

purpose of, 994, 995

reign of, 596

right of private judgment and, 117

Riswick, peace of, 477

William the Silent, 594, 749

Williams, Elisha
biographical information on, 52, 54

Essential Rights and Liberties of Protestants, 53–118

Williams, Roger, 328, 344, 344*n*, 345*n*

Winchester, Elhanan
biographical information on, 970, 972

Century Sermon on the Glorious Revolution, 971–1000

century sermons and, xxiii

Winthrop, John, 342*n*, 1546

Wisdom. *See also* Knowledge
external advantages and, 873

guarding against danger and, 1140

Jesus Christ as, 15

Paul and, 859

of Solomon, 16, 18, 891, 904

states' constitutions and, 958

Witherspoon, John
biographical information on, 530, 532

Dominion of Providence over the Passions of Men, 531–58

Wolfe, James, 213

Wolsey, Thomas, 1486*n*

Woman
bond-woman's versus free woman's children, 1033, 1035, 1050

chastity and, 1200, 1200–1201*n*

earth and, 513, 514

flood and, 511–14

neighboring powers of earth helping, 514–15

paganism and, 1195*n*

Protestantism and, 517

resistance of, 737, 740

serpent and, 498

as symbol for true church of Christ, 505, 509, 519, 524

wilderness and, 506–8, 516

The Wonderful Works of God Are to Be Remembered (Osgood), 1219–34

Woodrow, 719

Word, Jesus Christ as, 134

World. *See also* Earth
America as example of free government to, 1126

citizens of, 1012, 1025

destruction of, 1585

God as sovereign of, 611–12, 786–87, 794, 795, 796–804, 810–12

God as superintendent over, 793–94, 1221, 1315

opinion of, 1109–10

praise or censure of, 1109

Worship. *See also* Prayer; Religious
  liberty
  John Adams and, 1469
  authority and, 1015
  churches and, 963
  church-state relations and, 365–66
  conscience and, 97, 101–2, 644, 873
  French Revolution and, 1259
  God and, 1126
  gospel and, 1062
  government and, 873
  of heathens, 1197
  history of, 1256
  of Israel, 946, 948–49
  and laws of Jesus Christ, 69–71
  liberty of, 404
  liturgy, 1015, 1023*n*
  moral obligation to, 893–94
  national happiness and, 877–78
  neglect of, 831
  non-conformers to, 346
  peace within, 879–80
  public, 1116, 1381
  of reason, 1255–56, 1286
  right of private judgment and, 55,
    90
  Sabbath and, 1381
  scriptures and, 962
  support of, 348, 359, 1212
  Test Laws and, 1022
  United States and, 1438
  Washington and, 1469
Wortman, Tunis
  biographical information on, 1478,
    1480
  Griswold and, 1530
  Jefferson and, 1525
  Linn and, 1480, 1481–82
  *Solemn Address to Christians and
    Patriots,* 1479–1528

Wrath of men
  American Revolution and, 669–70,
    672
  as corruption of human nature,
    535–38
  Cumings's *Sermon Preached at
    Lexington on the 19th of April,*
    659–81
  God's praise and, 662, 666, 670,
    1180, 1331
  God's punishment and, 678–79
  God's restraint of, 666–70, 673,
    680, 1180
  perpetuation of, in human race,
    661–62
  repentance and, 538–41
  restraints to, 541–44
  revolutions and, 665, 669
Wright, Mr., 306
Wythe, George, 1306

Xenophon, 1201, 1202
Xerxes, 860, 1401
XYZ affair, 1340

York, archbishop of, 132
York, house of, 1297, 1510
York, Virginia, 781
Yorktown, 1391
Young, Doctor, 1401
Youth. *See also* Children; Parents
  dignity of man and, 906–7
  education of, 961–62, 1072–73, 1440
  infidelity and, 1472
  liberty and, 1074
  mortality and, 880
  religious education of, 1073–74
  subordination of, 1360*n*
Yule, 1258
Zebulun, 759

Zechariah, 188, 757
Zedekiah, 320, 321
Zeno, 1200, 1206
Zeruiah, sons of, 1426
Zidonians, 1134, 1143
Ziklag, 583, 755
Zion, 618, 625, 666, 762, 783, 813, 1567.
    See also Israel; Jews

Zizca, Captain, 747
Zubly, John Joachim
    biographical information on, 266
    *Humble Enquiry into the Nature of
    the Dependency of the American
    Colonies upon the Parliament of
    Great Britain,* 267–99, 422
Zuinglius, 204

Biblical Citation Index

OLD TESTAMENT

GENESIS 663

1:31 XIX*n*

4:10 590

4:19 333*n*

5:20 1455*n*

6:3 45

6:5–8:21 539*n*

6:13, 15 333*n*

7:11 1456*n*

7:19 1455*n*

8:21 333*n*

14:12 751

14:14, 19 751

19:17 590

31:24 590

49:14, 15 759

49:19 760

EXODUS 663

5:1 590

15:11 973

17:9, etc. 572

18:21 152*n*, 1325

19:4 507

20:10 1470*n*

23:2 1425*n*

23:15, 16 343*n*

31:3 18*n*

LEVITICUS

16 39

17:13 155*n*

19:15 153*n*

19:36 149*n*

25:14–17 589

25:44, 45, 46 1050

36 614

NUMBERS

14:28 401

25:17, 18 763

30:2 763

DEUTERONOMY

4:5–8 945

8:11, 12, 13, 14 839

13 340*n*

13:12, 15 763

16:16, 17 343*n*

16:18, 19 947

16:18, 19, 20 164*n*

19:16 153*n*

DEUTERONOMY, *continued*

20:10	755
23:20, 21	760
24:14, 15	155n
26	343n
26:20	139
27:25	787n
28	614
28:37, 44, 45	43
30:16	788n
32:4	584
32:5, 6, 15, 16	842n
32:10	616
32:15	42
32:36	616
32:43	611

JOSHUA

7:1	44
9	1050
10:12, 13, 14	1506

JUDGES

1:7	716
3:1, 2	751
3:8	751
3:10	751
3:14	751
4:1, 3	751
4:7	752
5:9	318
5:16, 17, 23	759
5:18, 19	759
5:20	195
8:22, etc.	753
9:23, 24, etc.	753

9:50	753
10:16	37
12	754
15:2	754
18:7	1133
19:20	570
20	13n, 14n, 763
20:23	571
20:26, etc.	571

I SAMUEL

2:8	11
2:12–16	346
7	42
8	1547
12:24	1309
14:44, 45	754
17:42, 43, 44, 45	548
22:2	755
23:13	755
24:10, 12, 13	727
24:15	588
26:9, 10	727
26:10	727
30:6	583

2 SAMUEL   668

3:38	1399
3:39	1426n
10:12	553
14:20	15n
20	755
21	441
23:3	141, 382, 860n, 1424n, 1469n
23:6	760

I KINGS

2:2	887
4:29	15n
11:28	1423n
12	664, 755
12:24	590

2 KINGS

2:12	858n
6:32	755
9:2	756
14:19	756
15:2	756
21:11, etc.	743

I CHRONICLES

12:1	755
16	1582
16:22	590
28:11–19	335
29:2	343n
29:12, 13	18

2 CHRONICLES

2:12	16
10	755
12:12	365
15:1, 2	211
15:2	49
15:7	50
15:15	38
20:1–3	34
20:20	33
21:10	756
23	756

25:27	756
26	756
28:1	315
28:19	315
28:22	315
31	343n
32:25	841n
36:16	40

EZRA

4	757
5:3, 5	757
6	757
6:6–9	343

NEHEMIAH

2:19, 20	757
4	757
6	757
9:2	39
9:27	618
9:38	37
10:29–31	37
13:10–13	343n

ESTHER 541, 665

3:8	352n
3:12, 13	758
9	758

JOB

5:17	619
12:17, 18	18n
15:31–35	679
19:21	716

JOB, *continued*

26:7	12*n*
34:29	44
38	13

PSALMS 573, 616, 888, 974

2:6, 8	187
2:10–12	336, 1475*n*
2:10, 11	385
8	xx
9:1, 4	773
9:17	1475*n*
11	1145
11:3	1427*n*
12:8	1425*n*
15:4	1469*n*
18	162
24:2	12*n*
33:15	18*n*
35:1	587
36:5, 6	16
44:5	766
44:9	766
46:1, 5	43
50	1582
51:17	34
54:4, 5	766
57	766
57:4	766
69:15	511
72:3	16
72:7, 11, 17	187
74:5, 6	534
74:10	661
74:13	500
74:22	544*n*, 583

75:3	14, 16
75:6, 7	18*n*, 1426*n*
76:10	533, 1445*n*
77:20	1105
78:34–36	38
78:34–37	844*n*
78:34	35, 540
78:69	1589
82	14
82:6, 7	1439*n*
84:8	42
93:1	1589
96:13	1578
105:15	590
105:45	123
106:15	856*n*
106:39	357*n*
107:38, 39	1419*n*
109:4	1221
110:1–3	187
110:5	1475*n*
115:16	57
119:134	xix*n*
122:2, etc.	1009
122:3	913
124	622, 1021
127:7, 8	238
130:1	35
140	587
140:7, 9	766
143	588
144:15	1189
146	587
146:6	584
149:6	768

PROVERBS

3:3	1466n
3:27, 28	154n
8:14	18n
8:15, 16	144n
11:1	48
14:34	42, 43, 854n
17:26	722
19:27	346n
20:6	16
21:30, 31	43
22:23	588
23	588
24:3, 4, 5	15n
24:11, 12	743, 763
29:25	1446n
31:4	1425n

ECCLESIASTES

7:2, 4	722
7:7	1427n
7:29	333n
8:8	1439n
9:18	44
10:1	1425n
10:5, 6, 7	1430n
10:16	1426n
10:20	722

CANTICLES

5:15	15

ISAIAH

	980, 1020, 1313n
1:3	1473n
1:5, 6	43
1:16, 17	36
1:17	764
1:19, 20	574, 869
1:23	764
2:2, 4	573
3:4, 5	1419
3:8	1426
8:12, 13	1446n
9:4	742
9:6, 7	187
10	666
10:5–19	541n
14:2, 3	760
22:12–14	34
23:17	499
26:8, 9	539
26:11	539
29:13	336
29:20, 21	353
30:1–3	1476n
30:9, 10	1476n
33	441
33:6	9
33:15, 16	49, 1446n
35:4	609
36	534
37	666
45:15	35
47:8	842n
49:13	619
49:23	1471n
49:26	619
51:9	500
55:6, 7	39
58:6	764
58:6, 8	47

ISAIAH, *continued*

58:8, 9	47
58:12	47
59:1, 2	36
59:9, 10, 12–14	46
59:14	1442n
59:18	609
59:19	511
60	620
60:2	1444n
63:1	200
65:8	45
66:8	775

JEREMIAH 1314n

2:19	44
2:20, 25	761
2:35	1438n
3:19	42
4	441
5:1	742–43
5:3	539, 584
5:9	1438n
17	316
18	316
18:7–10	793
18:7, 8	27, 32
18:7, etc.	614
19	316
22:3	164n
25:4	743
28:16	1186
30:20, 21	631
31:15	776n

31:18–20	41
36:2, 3	40
44:4	44
50:33–34	588
51:7	500
51:33, etc.	588
59:3	743

LAMENTATIONS 928

EZEKIEL

9:4, 5	41
14:6	37
16:49	842n
19:14	14
22:30	743
29:3	500
33:11	44
33:14, 15	41
33:31	729
35:25–28	45
37:21, 22, 24	187

DANIEL 1594

2:20	18n
2:21	18n
2:34, 35, 44	188
2:49	1470n
4:32	1426n
6:4–11	335
7:13, 14	188
8	1590
9:8	35
9:19	35

9:30, 34   761

10:12   506

11   744

HOSEA

2:5, 8   357n

6:1   38, 619

6:4   38

7:16   37

10:12   45

11:1–4   1419n

14:3   38

JOEL

2   1587

2:13   34

2:14   31

2:17   35

AMOS

3:2   30, 1438n

5:24   788n

OBADIAH

10   616

JONAH

2:10   29, 773

3:1   29

3:4   30

3:5   30

3:6   30

3:7   30

3:8   30

3:9   31

3:10   29, 31

MICAH

3:5, 9   346

3:11   1438n

4:3   538

4:11   762

6:8   38, 788n

7:3   315

7:8, etc.   588

HABAKKUK

3:2   43

HAGGAI

1:6–11   343n

2:17–19   343n

ZECHARIAH

1:19, 20   762

2:6   764

2:7   764

2:9   764

7:8, 10   39

9:9   188

9:13, 17   761

10:5, etc.   763

12:10   35

MALACHI

2:7   63

3:7–12   343n

NEW TESTAMENT

MATTHEW

2:2	188
2:18	776n
5:39	727
7:12	93, 101, 743
12:40	29
12:41	30
15:9	336
16:18	14
19:24	859n
22:21	53, 155n
23:1–9	337
23:8, 9, 10	81, 86, 87
23:9, 10	341
25:31, etc.	358n
26:52	573, 727, 728
26:53	195
27:16	189
28:19, 20	79
28:20	68
30:21	715

MARK

2:18, 20	34
7:7	89

LUKE

1:32, 33	189
1:74, 75	334n
9:49	340
9:56	201
10:3–16	337

10:10–12	358n
10:42	1026
11:32	31
12:20, 21	358n
12:21	343n
13:1	540
13:34	1026
18:37	94
19:10	201
22:25–27	337
22:36	764
22:36, 38	573
22:37	764
22:38	764
22:53	191

JOHN

3:21	351
5:43, 44	343
5:44	859n
7:48	859n
8:32	XVIn, 334n
8:33	XVIn, 36
9:39	1586
12:31	191, 1586
12:32	202
12:43	859n
13:20	358n
16:2	357n
17:2	189
18:11	728
18:36	729

18:36, 37	337
18:37	181, 183
19:12	352n
20:31	62
21:12, 25	1576

ACTS

1:6	188
2	1588
2:36	189
4:24, 28	542
5:31	189
7:8	340
17:11	63
17:26	1459n
22:28	374, 375
26:18	197

ROMANS

1:16	XXI
1:16	201
3:13–17	1430n
6:18	334n
8:36, 37	198
9:3	1026
11	205
11:15	775n
12:8	1422n
12:14–12	1533
12:17	727
13:1–5	21
13:1–10	336
13:1, 2	729
13:1, 77, 79	144n, 852n
13:2	144n, 722, 736, 739, 1432n

13:3, 4	80
13:4	144n, 561, 574, 1469n
13:5	144n
13:6	155n
14:5, 23	359
14:9	193
14:9, 10	86

I CORINTHIANS

1:21	1206n
1:24	15n
1:26	859n
4:5	357n
5:7, 8	155n
7:5	34
7:23	81, 86
9:11	366n
9:13, 14	340
10:15	63
12:21, 25	850n
14:40	89
15	1592

2 CORINTHIANS

1:12	353
2:14	198
3:17	86, 1153
4:2	353
4:4	191
4:17	198
5:10	356
5:14, 15	1474n
6:1, 2	546
7:10	35

2 CORINTHIANS, *continued*

10:3–5	196
10:3, 5	191

GALATIANS

2:9	14
4:16	1476n
4:31	86, 1033
5:1	81, 84, 85, 86, 1061
5:13	86, 329
6:6	366n
6:6, 7	340

EPHESIANS

1:21, 22	189
1:22	190
2:3	191
2:20	14
6:10–18	196
6:12	191

PHILIPPIANS

2:9–11	189
2:10	336
4:6	1466n
4:9, 10	366n
4:18	356

COLOSSIANS

2	337
2:3	15n
2:15	191
2:20, 22	335
3:17	1466n
3:17, 23	336
4:17	358n

1 THESSALONIANS

5:17, 18	1343
5:21	63

2 THESSALONIANS

2:4	526
2:11, 12	854n

1 TIMOTHY

2:1, 2	729
5:17, 18	366n
6:6, 9	331
6:12	196

2 TIMOTHY

1:13, 14	819
2:3	196
2:12	201
2:26	191
3:1, 2	49
3:15, 16	62
4:3, 4	819
4:7	196
6:13	186

TITUS

2:14	855n
3:1	21, 1432n
3:3	334
3:11	344, 344n

HEBREWS

1:14	191
2:14	191
2:6–12	XX
3:5	72

11:6	33
11:7	33
12:7, 17	366n
12:11	538
13:15, 16	366
13:16–18	356
13:17, 77, 78	358n

JAMES

1:14, 15	333n
1:17	18n
1:25	XVIn
2:12	XVIn
4:1	116, 537
5:16	35

1 PETER

2:11	333n
2:13	723, 1432n
2:13, 14	335
2:13, 14, 15, 16, 17	21
2:14	574
2:16	XVIn
2:21	728
4:10, 11	340

2 PETER

2:18	334

1 JOHN

4:1, 63	1368
4:2, 3, 6	1369n
5:4	198
5:13	62

2 JOHN

10:11	346n

REVELATION | 573

1:6	201
1:18	193
2:5	40
3:12	22
3:21	201
4:1	498
5:12	189
6:9	519
7:14	198
11:3, 5	521
11:10	519
12	499, 1590
12:1	505
12:2	505
12:6	509
12:7	506
12:7, 9	195
12:11	198
12:14	505
12:14–17	494
12:14, 15, 16, 17	497
12:15	511
12:16	513
12:17	516
13	494, 500, 501, 524
13:1	525
13:2	93
13:4	520
13:5	527
13:10	728
13:11	525